Ben Hunt's
BIG BOOK OF WHITTLING

Ben Hunt's
BIG BOOK OF WHITTLING

MACMILLAN PUBLISHING CO., INC.
NEW YORK

COLLIER MACMILLAN PUBLISHERS
LONDON

To Laura

Compiled from *Ben Hunt's Whittling Book* Copyright 1944 by W. Ben Hunt and *More Ben Hunt Whittlings* Copyright 1947 by W. Ben Hunt.

Library of Congress Catalog Card Number: 78–140901

MACMILLAN PUBLISHING CO., INC.
866 THIRD AVENUE, NEW YORK, NEW YORK 10022
COLLIER MACMILLAN CANADA, INC.

14 13 12 11 10 9 8 7 6 5

Printed in the United States of America

Table of Contents

FACES, FIGURES, AND FUN

SPECIAL PROJECTS

Introduction

Whittling is really carving with a knife. The word "whittling" is used mainly in the United States; in other countries the word "carving" is used. Wonderful carvings have been made by primitive craftsmen who used only the crudest knives. These works, probably because of their great beauty, are called carvings. Nevertheless, since they were carved with a knife, they are examples of whittling: the good old American term "whittling" applies whenever knives instead of carving tools are used.

Whittling is an inexpensive and clean hobby. The kitchen, the basement, the garage, the outdoors, and even some room in a city apartment can be a whittler's workshop. What could be better than sitting in the shade of a tree or in a cozy corner of the kitchen with a sharp knife, a piece of wood, and an interesting project to be whittled? Because it is a hobby, some people think of whittling as only a form of amusement. Actually it is a skilled craft. Once learned, it can give you much satisfaction, and the interesting and attractive objects you will make will last for years.

We will be talking mainly about whittling wood, but other materials—such as plastics, bone, and fruit stones—can also be whittled.

In woodworking—fine carpentry or rustic construction— there are few tools as useful as the ordinary pocketknife. It is one of the simplest of hand tools: it isn't hard to sharpen; it is always ready for a variety of uses; and it is safe and easy to carry. The beginning whittler should buy a moderately priced pocketknife and an oilstone for sharpening it. When the knife is ready the next question is usually "What shall I make?"

The projects illustrated and described in this book were selected because they were of interest to many craft and hobby enthusiasts. They are intended only as a basis for developing and guiding the beginner's own creativity and self-expression.

The projects have been arranged in order of difficulty within each subject grouping. The easiest of the bird projects comes first, the easiest of the animals before the more difficult, and the beginning "Faces, Figures, and Fun" projects before the more exacting jobs.

There are thousands of exciting objects to whittle that are not included. For example, I have received many requests for elaborate projects such as Christmas crib sets. The reasons for not including such items are two: few people who need the experience of making the other projects would go to the trouble of making a large and complex grouping; still fewer would be able to take on the difficult task of a crib set because it would require so many individual pieces.

If you like to whittle as a hobby, don't be discouraged if you do not find exactly what you want in this or another book. This is the time to tackle something original—then whittling becomes really interesting. Once you have mastered the basic skills, you can pick your own subject. The ones you choose yourself may well be not only the most difficult and challenging but the most satisfying of all. Don't hesitate to whittle on your own!

BEN HUNT'S BIG BOOK OF WHITTLING

Getting Started

1 The Best Knife for You

Four things are needed for good whittling: a good knife, an oilstone or whetstone, a good piece of wood, and an idea of what to make. First, we will take up the question of knives.

A pocket knife, or jackknife, is all you need to start whittling. Later on, a few specially shaped knives will come in very handy. When you buy a pocket-knife, remember that good steel costs more than poor steel. A good knife usually has brass side plates, strong rivets, and stiff springs. The rivets prevent the blade from becoming wobbly, and the springs keep it from closing while cutting. The grade of steel in a knife is never known until the knife has been tried. Good steel means that a blade should stay sharp for a long time with ordinary whittling on soft woods. The edge should not bend over or chip when a knot is struck.

Fancy handles do not make good knives. The handle should be smooth and from 3 to 3½ inches in length. A three-bladed knife is ideal (see Figure 1). The large blade, shown in Figure 2, is used for heavy or rough cutting, and the small blades, shown in Figure 3, for close work. This knife will cost from three to six dollars.

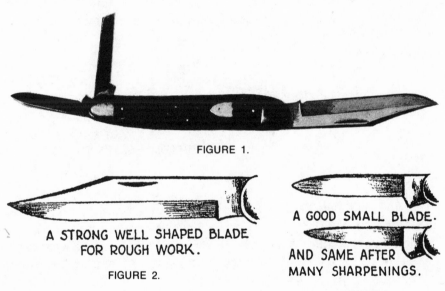

FIGURE 1.

A STRONG WELL SHAPED BLADE
FOR ROUGH WORK.

FIGURE 2.

A GOOD SMALL BLADE.

AND SAME AFTER
MANY SHARPENINGS.

FIGURE 3.

Figure 4 shows a good two-blade knife. A lot more can, and will, be done with the small blade, rather than the large blade shown in Figure 5. This is where the quality of the steel will be tested: the small blade must be able to take the strain put on it. But the best of steel will break with careless handling.

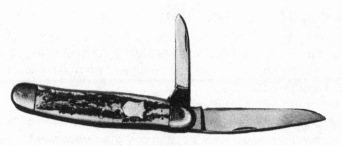

FIGURE 4.

A LARGE THIN BLADE FOR
ALL-AROUND WORK.

FIGURE 5.

Other Knives You Can Make or Buy

Another handy knife to have is the skew knife (see Figure 6). It can easily be made of a piece of steel, such as a power hacksaw blade or a flat drill rod, or even by carefully grinding down a flat file or a broken palette knife, as shown in Figure 7.[1]

FIGURE 6.

SMALL SKEW KNIFE MADE
FROM BROKEN PALETTE KNIFE.

FIGURE 7.

The sloyd knife (see Figure 8) is a very fine knife for whittling because it will not close while cutting and is usually made of a better grade of steel than the ordinary pocketknife. The blade shown in Figure 9 is a bit wide for fine work, but it is suitable for making such objects as the Kachina dolls in Chapter 21.

FIGURE 8.

[1]See *Ben Hunt's Big Indiancraft*, W. Ben. Hunt, The Bruce Publishing Company, New York, N.Y., for making the crooked and skew knife.

SHORT BLADED SLOYD KNIFE.

FIGURE 9.

Many carvers prefer the reground desk knife, shown in the two parts of Figure 10. The knife has a solid handle, and it can be made by grinding down an old paper, or desk, knife.

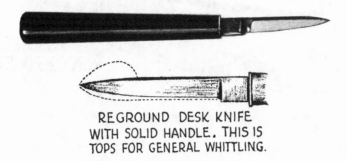

REGROUND DESK KNIFE
WITH SOLID HANDLE. THIS IS
TOPS FOR GENERAL WHITTLING.

FIGURE 10.

The Eskimos and the west coast Indians made knives of many different shapes which they used for different purposes. They made knives of iron or steel with curved blades. These are called crooked knives (see Figure 11). Although the Indian actually does not do a great deal of whittling as we know it, he uses his knife to make birchbark canoes and to whittle paddles, bowls, and ladles. The Eskimo uses his crooked knife to whittle bone, wood, and ivory. The Eskimos and the west coast Indians are good craftsmen.

FIGURE 11.

A small crooked knife with a blade about 2 or $2\frac{1}{4}$ inches long, as shown in Figure 12, takes the place of the wood-carver's gouge. One can easily be made from a piece of tool steel or a small knife blade.

If you do a lot of whittling you will occasionally cut your fingers; but remember, if the knife is held correctly, this is less likely to happen.

You will also find that in the beginning your hands will tire very quickly. Blisters will form, especially at the inner side of the second joint of the index finger. The thin leather band shown in Figure 13 will make things much easier. If your hands tire and blister, stop a while and let them rest. After a few hours of whittling and resting, your hands will toughen up for working at this delightful old Yankee pastime—whittling.

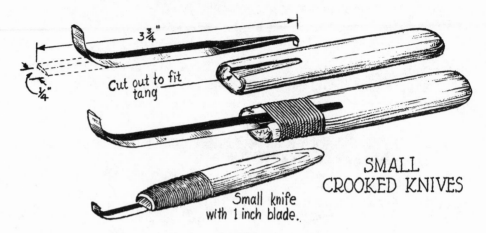

3¾"

Cut out to fit tang

¼

SMALL
CROOKED KNIVES

Small knife
with 1 inch blade.

FIGURE 12.

FIGURE 13.

2 How to Sharpen Your Knife

It is important that a knife keep its sharp edge, but first you must give it an edge. Most people do this with an oilstone, and it is probably the best way. I prefer a good whetstone, because water is always handy, but fine oil is not always available. A good stone has a coarse surface on one side and a fine surface on the other. If a stone has only one surface, it should be fine. To sharpen a knife, lay the blade flat on the stone and then raise the back of the blade very slightly. Raising it too high forms a chisel edge which will not do for whittling. (See Figure 14.)

Draw the knife back and forth over the stone, first one side and then the other (see Figure 15), until the edge cannot be seen or until a fine wire edge appears. This is removed either by stropping on a good strop (see Figures 16 and 17), or on a buffing wheel. The strop or the wheel should be dressed with a buffing compound.

For a razor-sharp edge, a leather strop fastened to a piece of wood is necessary. This removes the wire edge and gives the edge the proper finish. A strip of very fine emery or Carborundum cloth about $1\frac{1}{2}$ or $1\frac{3}{4}$ inches wide, tacked to a piece of wood of the same width, also makes ideal sharpening equipment. When you are using the sharpening stick, the blade should be drawn only one way, and in the same manner as in honing (see Figures 16 and 17).

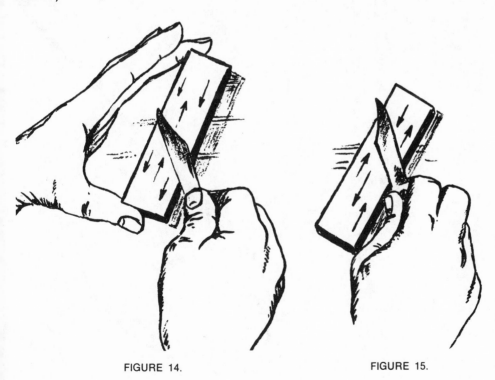

FIGURE 14.   FIGURE 15.

Although a beginner is apt to cut himself more easily with a sharp knife, he cannot whittle successfully with a dull knife. Also, there is less danger of a sharp blade slipping.

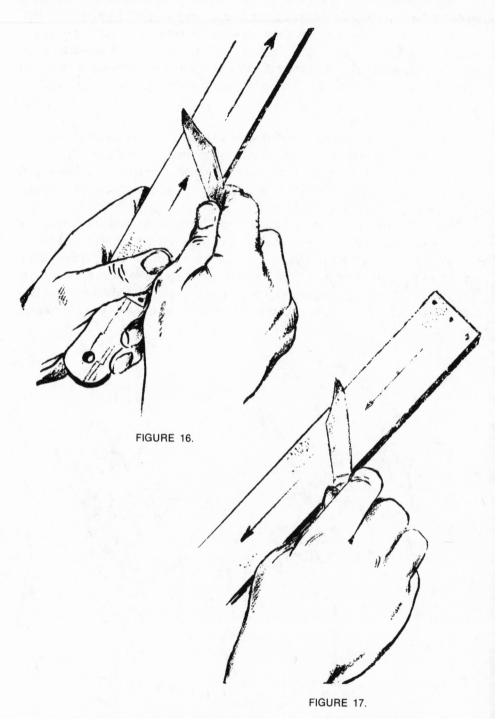

FIGURE 16.

FIGURE 17.

3 Using a Pocketknife

In whittling, as in any craftwork, the first thing to learn is how to hold the tools. A knife must be held firmly. Place the knife in the hand as shown in Figure 18, then close the fingers over the handle. The back of the blade should be set firmly in the crotch formed by the index finger and thumb, as shown in Figure 19. The handle should not show. Then lock the thumb over

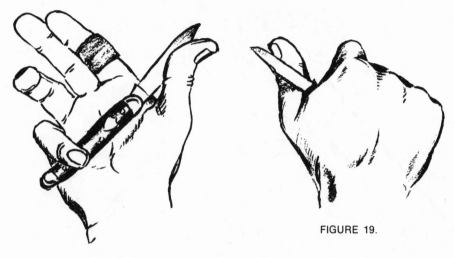

FIGURE 19.

FIGURE 18.

the index finger, bringing the handle of the knife tightly against the middle of the palm. The thumb should not be placed on the back of the blade for cutting during whittling, except for special work.

Figure 20 shows the firm grip that is to be used for all rough whittling.

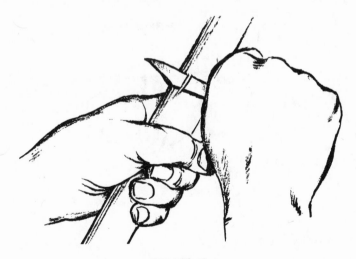

FIGURE 20.

The left hand, with which the wood is usually held, should always be away from the cutting edge. When it is necessary to cut toward yourself, the wood should be held as is shown in Figure 21. In this manner the cut can be better controlled than when you are cutting away from yourself. Figure 20 shows how to hold the wood for making long cuts; Figure 21 shows how to hold the wood for making short cuts.

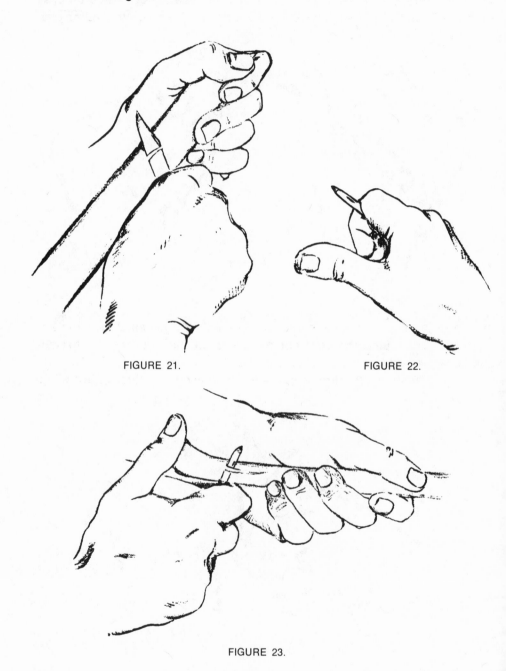

FIGURE 21.

FIGURE 22.

FIGURE 23.

Figure 22 shows how a knife is held for fine cutting. Notice how the forefinger closes around the base of the blade. When you are holding the knife this way, there is no danger of cutting your finger, because the blade lies flat.

The thumb may be used as a steady rest and help to pull the blade when you are cutting (see Figure 23). The thumb plays an important part in whittling.

Figure 24 shows how the thumb is used on the back of the blade. In this position it is applied in a pushing motion for cutting notches or cutting straight down into the wood. The stick, in this case, is usually rested on the knee.

Figure 25 shows how the thumb is used to steady and pull the blade. In fine whittling, the thumb is placed on some part of the wood, sometimes to steady the blade and sometimes to help pull the blade through the wood.

Figure 26 shows the simplest and best method used for cutting spirals (see chapter on whittling spirals, page 163). Whittle the full length of the spiral first on one side, then reverse the stick and cut the other side. This action is repeated until the proper depth of the cut has been reached. In this way you have control of the blade at all times.

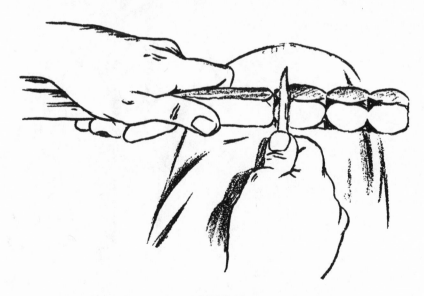

FIGURE 24.

The thumb may also be used to push the blade (see Figure 21). It is helpful when the grain of the wood is crooked, and when a careful cut is required. Notice that only as much of the blade as necessary projects beyond the clamp of the forefinger (see Figure 26).

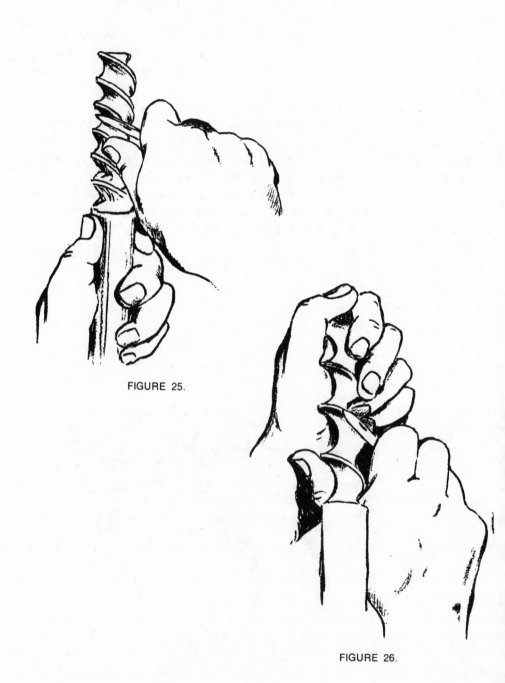

FIGURE 25.

FIGURE 26.

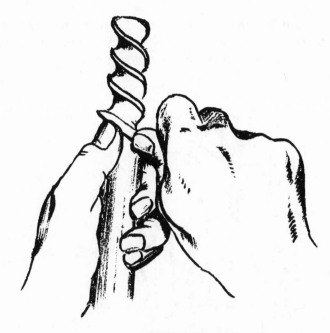

FIGURE 27.

FIGURE 28.

The method for making a deep cut is shown in Figure 28. If this method is not used carefully, a small blade may very easily be broken off. The wood should rest on your knee or a table. As there is no thumb here to steady or regulate the cut, care should be taken when you are cutting near the edge of the wood, so that the blade does not slip and injure your knee.

Figures 29 and 30 show two methods of making the same cut with less danger of slipping. Remember that although the thumb is a wonderful steady rest, and helps in many ways during whittling, it is not a very good stop for a sharp blade!

FIGURE 29.

FIGURE 30.

4 Woods for Whittling

Softwood is best for whittling. I think that Wisconsin and Michigan white pine is probably the most suitable, because it is free of knots, has very little grain, and is inexpensive. This wood is becoming scarce, however, and sugar pine is often used in its place. Sometimes choice pieces of white pine can be salvaged from old houses that are being torn down. Other soft pines work well also. Wood for whittling should be free of pitch.

If white pine is not available, the next choice is linden, also called basswood, seasoned or green. This is harder than pine, but it has a fine texture and is quite tough. Both dry and green poplar are also very good. The Hopi Indians of the southwest carve cottonwood branches and roots to make their Kachina dolls. Cottonwood is very similar to poplar. Poplar is used for crate lumber, but it can also be obtained in planks two inches thick, or thicker.

If possible, when you are whittling round objects, use green basswood, poplar, willow, or box elder—in fact, any native wood that contains no pitch or resin. These woods are easy to cut to shape, and this helps to raise the beginner's confidence.

As we have said anyone starting to whittle, especially for the first time, will be surprised how quickly his hands tire and become sore. Therefore, the softest woods should be used at first (except for balsa wood, which is not recommended because it is too soft).

5 Bark Whittling

Probably the simplest and easiest kind of whittling, and a very good project for beginners, is bark whittling as shown in Figure 31. You make a design by cutting away certain portions of bark from saplings or branches.

Any kind of wood with a smooth bark will do—the thinner the bark, the better. The saplings or branches for bark whittling should not be cut in early spring when the sap is running. At this time, the bark is too readily removed, and the bark you want left on the branch to create the design is likely to come off. Wood is ideal for bark whittling when there is little or no sap running—that is, any time after spring or early summer.

You will do well to cut and dry all saplings and branches before whittling. The bark will stick tightly to the wood once it is dried. Cut straight down through the bark to the wood and whittle out the sections to be removed. When the branches are dry, or partly dry, you can make slanting cuts for special designs.

Bark whittling is a simple form of the craft and is used mainly for decoration. You can decorate hiking staffs, canes, paper knives, and neckerchief slides. The Indians decorated their willow beds with bark whittling.

FIGURE 31. A few suggested designs for bark whittling.

6 Relief Carving – Birds

"What shall I whittle?" That is the one question that most beginners ask. It is best to start with something small that can be made in a short time; I suggest relief carving as a good project for a beginner. Figure 32 shows a duck carved in relief, and Figure 33 shows a duck in relief without a background.

Use carbon paper to trace and transfer the figure to a soft wood board ½ by 4 by 5 inches. Make a vertical cut all the way around the figure of the duck; cut away the background all around the edge of the figure and then cut away the entire background. These last two steps are shown in Figure 34. An Indian crooked knife is handy for removing the background.

After the background is smoothed, round the body contour and cut the feathers as shown in Figure 32. When whittling birds in relief, be sure to cut the off wing – that is, the wing on the far side – down to about half the thickness of the wing in the foreground. This gives it the proper perspective.

A flock of ducks or geese in various positions can be cut out of ¼-inch bass or pine board with a jigsaw or coping saw and whittled in relief. They can then be painted in natural colors and used for a wall decoration. Studies of birds, often with full-color illustrations, can be found in many of the bird books in the libraries and museums. A series of ducks (Figures 46 to 48) begins on page 31 of this book.

FIGURE 32. A simple bird carving.

FIGURE 33. The duck in relief without a background.

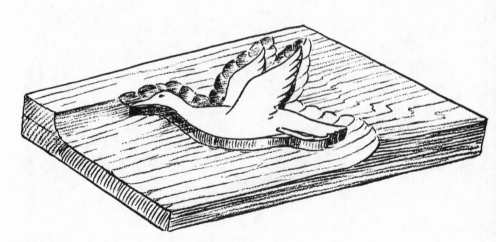

FIGURE 34. Cutting away the background.

7 Laying Out and Roughing Out

Now we are ready to begin a real whittling project. This is a plan for whittling a small bird. First, draw or transfer the outline onto the block and in such a way as to take advantage of the long grain of the wood, as shown in A, Figure 35. Whittling with the grain is easier than whittling against it.

Then cut away the larger portions of the unwanted wood. If possible, this should be done with a power saw. That does not make whittling any less a hand project but is merely a timesaving procedure. If you do not have a power saw, use a hand coping saw or a regular carpenter's saw. (A jigsaw, band saw, or fretsaw can also be used.) But if you don't have any of these saws, you will have to do it with your knife as a lot of primitive carvers do. The result is called a silhouette block, and it will look like B, Figure 35.

To aid in shaping the project, draw a center line down the front of the silhouette block as shown in C, Figure 35. Turn the block around and draw a line on the other side (D, Figure 35). Perhaps you will hit the center of the project the first time. If not, the true center will be found halfway between the two lines, as shown in E, Figure 35. Later on, in more advanced projects, it will be necessary for the center line to be off-center or curved, depending on the top view—if the bird's head were turned to one side, for instance.

Next, with a piece of paper or divider, measure off the width of the different parts, such as the beak, the head, the body, and the end of the tail. Draw the top view roughly, using these points as a guide, and the block will look like G, Figure 35. Also mark off the lines on the bottom as shown in F, Figure 35. Only a few minutes work is required to cut away the corners and edges, as shown in H, Figure 35. From then on it is quite simple to round out the various parts of the project.

These steps of laying out and roughing out should be used on all of the projects which follow.

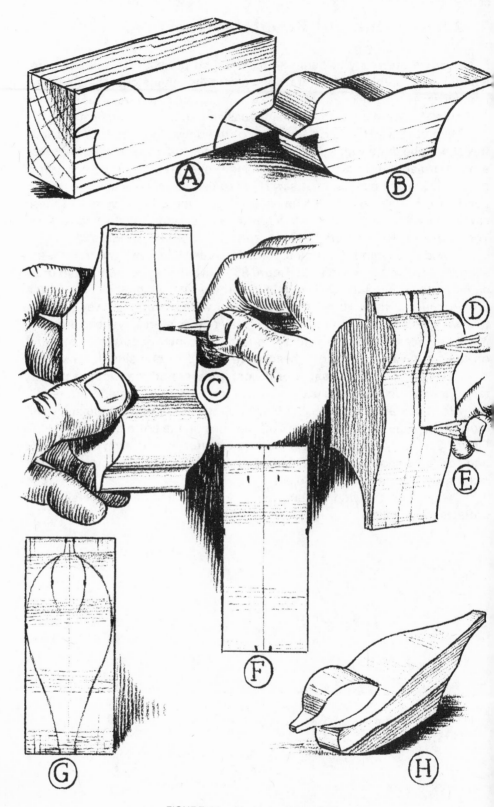

FIGURE 35.   Marking off the block.

My Favorite Birds

8 A Funny Duck

The funny little duck shown in Figure 36, is not at all difficult to whittle. Use patterns in Figure 38. Figure 37 shows how the side view is drawn on the block and how most of the wood can be cut away with an ordinary hand-saw. Figure 37 also shows the block roughed out and ready for rounding and finishing. Full-size patterns for the front, side, and rear views can be seen in Figure 38.

This little duck looks fine after it is painted. Mark the areas to be painted with a pencil. Paint the beak, feet, and eyes orange, the head green, and the band at the neck yellow or white. Allow each color to dry thoroughly before applying the next. Then the breast is painted buff or light brown, and the wings, back, and tail a dark brown. Watercolor gives this duck a matt finish, but enamels may be used if you want a shiny finish.

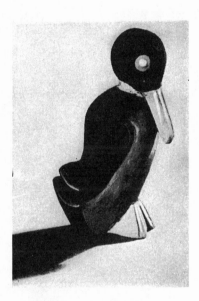

FIGURE 36.   The finished duck.

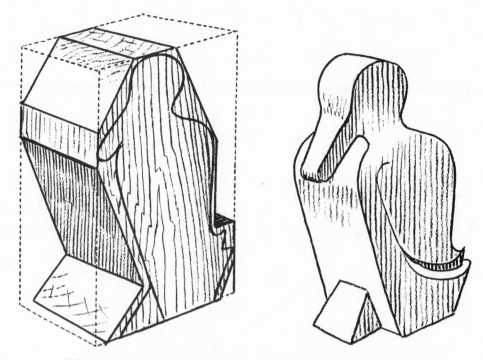

FIGURE 37. The block marked off, roughed out, and ready for finishing.

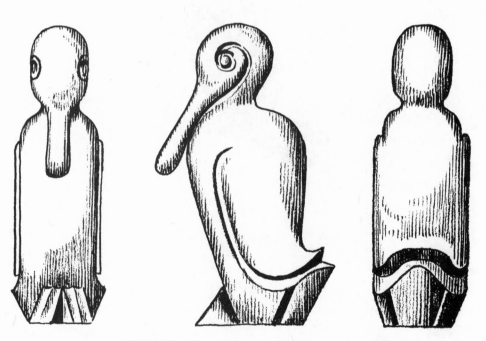

FIGURE 38. Front, side, and rear view of duck.

9 Miniature Decoy Ducks

Birds are always attractive ornaments because of their graceful lines and beautiful colors. A whittler can never have too many of them in his collection of whittlings. I hope that you will find the bird projects in this volume both colorful and interesting.

The miniature decoy ducks shown in Figure 39 look well on a shelf, and they can be used as paperweights. These three ducks are the types often used for decoys by duck hunters.

FIGURE 39. Miniature decoy ducks. Top, mallard drake; center, canvasback drake; bottom, pintail drake.

White pine or basswood is recommended for the ducks. It should be 1¾ inches thick.

The colors are indicated on Figures 40, 41, and 42, but it is best that you refer to some bird book with colored illustrations for the correct shades. Decoy ducks, as a rule, are painted in bold masses without the delicate shadings generally used in coloring a whittled object.

First, cut out the silhouette. You may saw the top-view outline, but since these ducks are so small, it takes only a few minutes to rough them out with a knife. The edges are then cut away, and the duck is ready for rounding and finishing with sandpaper. A flat, single-cut mill file is excellent for smoothing the bodies before sanding.

If these ducks are to be used for paperweights, two or three holes should be bored into the base from below. Using your knife, undercut the holes and fill them with molten lead. The undercutting prevents the lead from falling out. Cement a piece of felt over the entire bottom so that the finished surfaces upon which the paperweights are set down will not be marred. The patterns shown are smaller than full-sized, but can be enlarged and used for any size duck.

Watercolors or artist's oil paints can be used for coloring. If oil paints are used, the job is finished when the colors have dried. In the case of watercolors, however, a coat or two of white shellac or clear lacquer should be applied to prevent the birds from being soiled by dust and handling. You will discover that many persons prefer the dull, velvetlike appearance of watercolors to the shiny, glasslike finish of lacquer. They complain that lacquer makes a whittling look like porcelain.

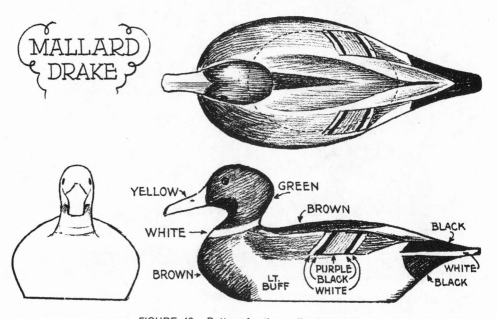

FIGURE 40. Pattern for the mallard drake.

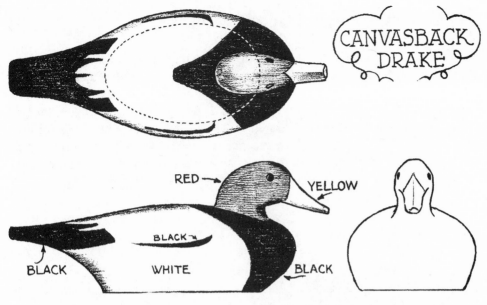

CANVASBACK DRAKE

RED YELLOW

BLACK

BLACK WHITE BLACK

FIGURE 41. Pattern for the canvasback drake.

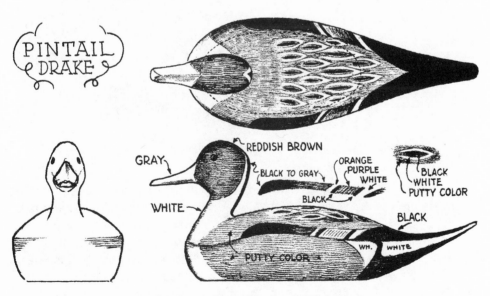

PINTAIL DRAKE

REDDISH BROWN

GRAY

BLACK TO GRAY

ORANGE
PURPLE
WHITE

BLACK
WHITE
PUTTY COLOR

WHITE

BLACK

BLACK

WH. WHITE

PUTTY COLOR

FIGURE 42. Pattern for the pintail drake.

10   Ducks for Wall Decorations

The whittling project shown in Figure 43 will be especially interesting to duck hunters. Three pairs of ducks are shown, and each pair may be colored differently, so that the project will represent a flock of various kinds of ducks. It is impossible to show colors here, and it is suggested that the whittler go to the library and look through books of birds for the coloring. Use watercolors and a couple of coats of clear lacquer (clear fingernail polish will do just as well) for finishing. All the ducks shown are whittled half in relief and half in the round, one side being left flat as the wall side.

FIGURE 43.   The entire flock.

Figure 44 shows progressive steps from the silhouette to the sanded finish. Figure 45 shows all the ducks after being sanded. All wing and tail feathers should be shown with rather fine V cuts. In making the green-winged teal, be sure to flatten its back as shown in Figure 46. This puts the duck in a better perspective. If its back is not flattened, the bird will look as if it were flying by flapping its wings alternately. Figure 43 shows the way a flock of whittled ducks may be hung on a wall.

Basswood or birch should be used for these ducks, as too soft a wood will be likely to break off at the ends of the feathers. Since these ducks are usually viewed straight on, a certain amount of thickness may be allowed in the wings and the wing feathers. The grain of the wood should run the long way, although if birch is used, it will not matter much which way it runs.

FIGURE 44. From silhouette to finished duck.

FIGURE 45.   The ducks ready for their colors.

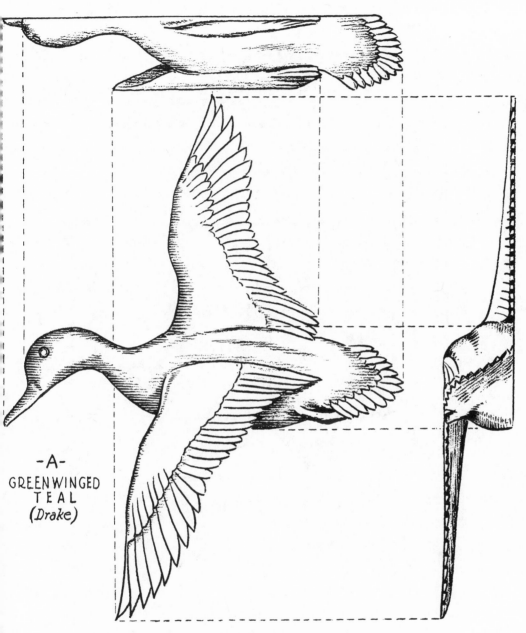

-A-
GREEN WINGED
T E A L
(Drake)

FIGURE 46A.   A pair of green-winged teals.   All patterns are full-size.

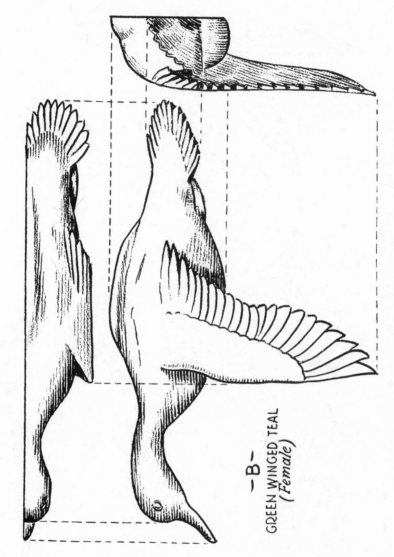

—B—
GREEN WINGED TEAL
(*Female*)

FIGURE 46B. A pair of green-winged teals. All patterns are full-size.

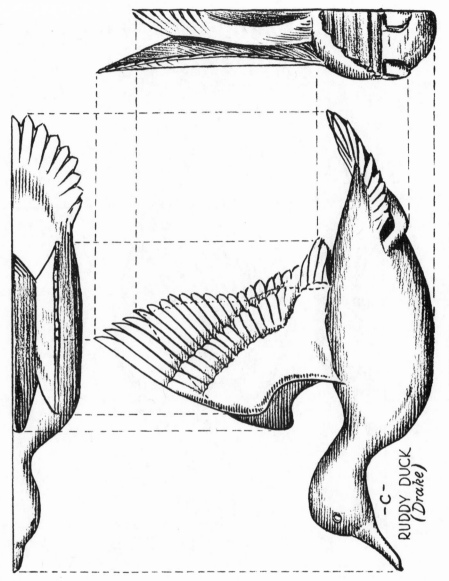

-C-
RUDDY DUCK
(Drake)

FIGURE 47A.   A pair of ruddy ducks.

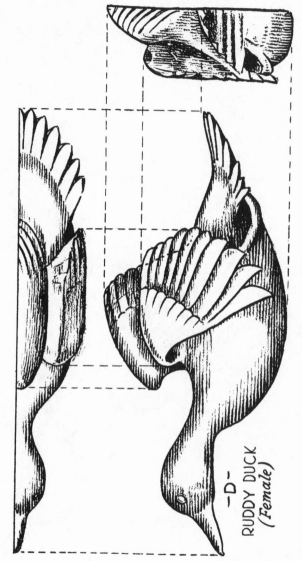

-D-
RUDDY DUCK
(Female)

FIGURE 47B. A pair of ruddy ducks.

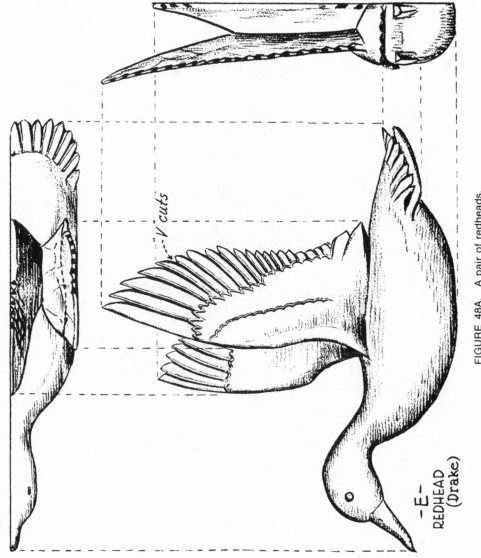

"V" cuts

-E-
REDHEAD
(Drake)

FIGURE 48A. A pair of redheads.

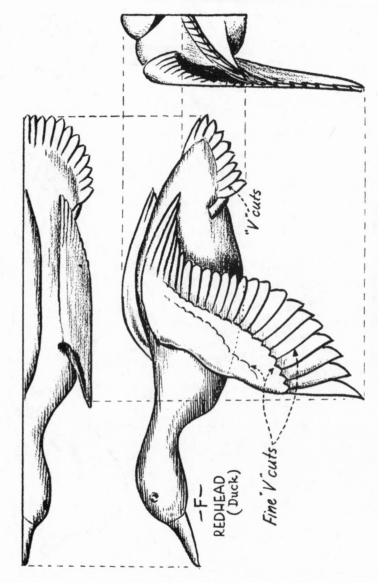

"V" cuts

Fine "V" cuts

—F—
REDHEAD
(Duck)

FIGURE 48B. A pair of redheads.

11   Richardson's Owl

The owl is whittled separately and then mounted, with two small brads, on a piece of dry branch.   Cut out the side-view silhouette in Figure 50 and then round up the figure.   After sanding, drill holes into the branch for the brads and put a drop or two of cement where the bird is to rest.   If you have a suitable piece of wood from which a stump for the base can be whittled, you will not have to search for a branch.   If a natural branch is used, it is suggested that you do not remove the bark.   A whittled stump can be painted a weathered grey color with a touch of moss green here and there for a natural effect.

Try to find a colored picture of a Richardson's owl in a bird book.   If you cannot find one, a fairly good job of painting can be done by making the body of the owl brown and white.   The photograph (Figure 49) shows how the colors are applied.   The face is white and grey.   The beak is black, and the eyes are yellow with black pupils.

FIGURE 49.   Richardson's owl.

FIGURE 50. Pattern for the Richardson's owl.

12 Female Cardinal

You must see this bird, or at least a good colored picture of it, to appreciate its beauty. Not as brightly colored as the male, the female cardinal is nevertheless delightfully shaded in delicate tones of orange and brown which it would be almost impossible to describe in words. Therefore, when it is time to paint the whittling, find a good colored illustration of the female cardinal to work from. Accentuate the colors when you paint your bird.

FIGURE 51. Two views of the female cardinal.

A piece of wood 1¾ inches thick is required for this bird. Pine is recommended. Saw out the silhouette as shown in the side view in Figure 52. Then sketch the profile of the head on the front of the silhouette as shown in the small sketch, with the end of the beak coming right to the edge. If you wish to have your bird looking over its right shoulder, sketch the head the opposite way. To have it looking straight ahead, make a silhouette combining the head of the front view and the body of the side view.

The female cardinal is a relatively simple job of whittling. It is a lot easier to carve than the male bird. After watching a pair of feeding cardinals, almost everyone will agree that the little lady is every bit as pretty as her mate and is well worth whittling.

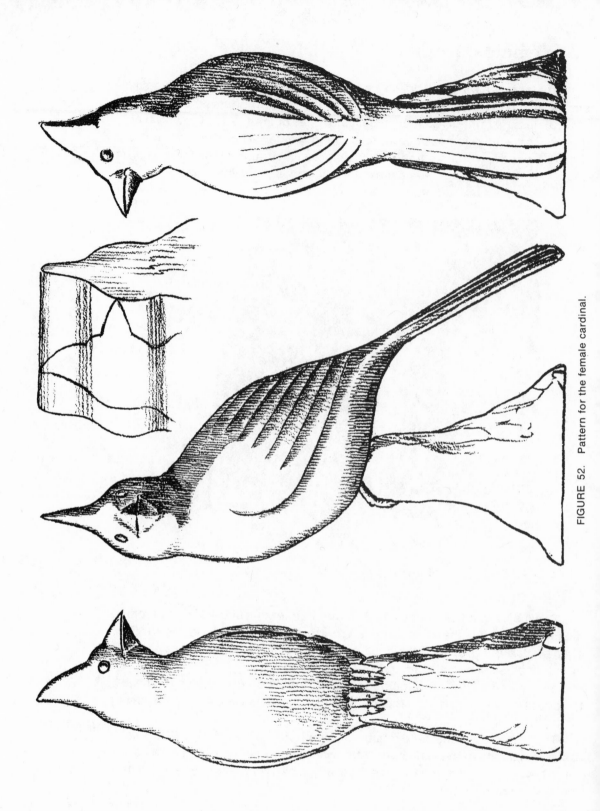

FIGURE 52. Pattern for the female cardinal.

13 Male Cardinal

For whittling the male cardinal shown in Figure 53, a piece of wood 2¼ by 5¾ inches will be required. However, if the wings are not spread—that is, if they are kept close to the body—a piece of wood 1½ inches thick will do.

FIGURE 53. Male cardinal.

Since this project is to be painted, two pieces of wood can be glued together to obtain the thickness required, and the joint will not be noticeable. In fact, it may be better to glue two good pieces of wood together than to try to whittle the bird from one solid piece which has defects. The bird shown in Figure 53 was whittled from a solid piece of pine which had a knot in it. As a result, it was necessary to do a lot of cutting against troublesome grain.

In whittling birds, you must handle the legs in such a way that they will not break. In this case the difficulty was overcome by having the bird rest on a sort of rough pedestal. The entire left leg is visible, and the right foot projects from under the bird's body (see Figure 54). If you want to make the whittling life-size, the actual length of a cardinal is 8¾ inches.

The grain, instead of running up and down, follows the beak and also nearly follows the tail feathers. As a result, there is almost no short grain to break off (see Figure 54).

Instead of the V cut to show the feathers, the author used the type of cut illustrated in the small sketch below the bird's head in Figure 54. A straight cut is made first, and then a long slant cut which meets it.

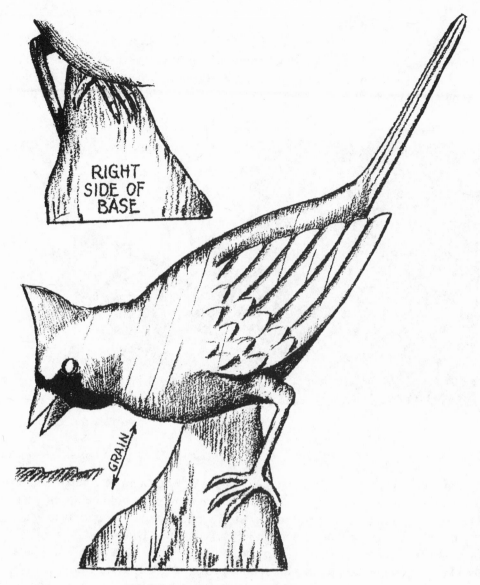

FIGURE 54.   Side view of the male cardinal.

For the coloring, it is best to refer to the pictures in a book on birds, but a satisfactory effect can be obtained by painting the entire body a bright red, the beak a light orange, and the legs a yellowish brown. The area about the beak is a solid black, as shown in our illustrations. The stump, or pedestal, can be made a greyish green to set off the bird.

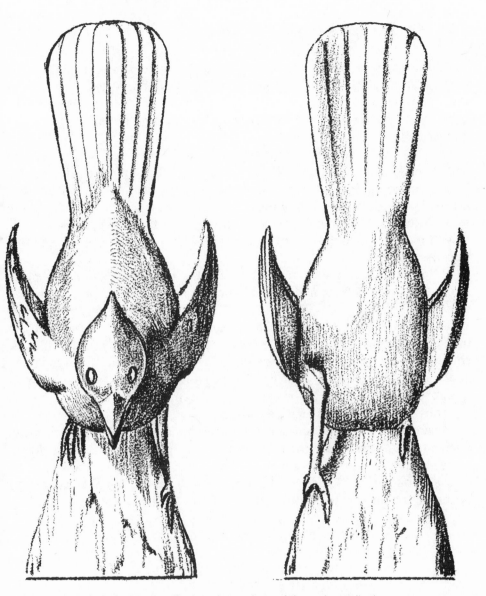

FIGURE 55.   Front and rear views of the male cardinal.

14 Bird Sticks — Kingfisher

For those who like bird sticks, here is a chance to do a real whittling job which will far surpass those jigsawed out of plywood. The whittled birds really look lifelike, regardless of which way they are facing. Most of the larger birds, such as robins and cardinals, can be whittled out of wood two inches thick.

Since I live in the country, I have enough real birds around my house, but I made the kingfisher shown in Figure 56 to guard the outdoor goldfish pond. There are too many visits from real kingfishers, for whom the small goldfish are real delicacies, and the whittled and very realistic kingfisher tends to scare others of his kind off. A kingfisher, as a rule, takes complete charge of a certain territory along a lake or river, and woe to any other of his kind that trespasses.

In order to trace the kingfisher in full size, enlarge the design on a piece of paper, marking off the squares as indicated in Figure 58. Sandpaper it as shown in Figure 57.

To color the kingfisher, give the entire body a coat of white paint and then paint the parts, as outlined in Figure 58, in a bluish grey. The bill, eyes, shoulder spots, wing tips, and feet should be painted black. After the paint is dry, apply two coats of spar varnish to protect the bird against weather.

Other birds that you may wish to make can easily be traced or copied from one of the many bird books available.

Usually birds for garden sticks are mounted on a ³⁄₈-inch birch dowel fitted into a ³⁄₈-inch hole in the feet. But for the kingfisher, a hole was drilled crosswise through the feet, and a round stick was glued into it to give a more natural appearance. Then the birch dowel was fitted into the hole, illustrated by the dotted lines at the bottom of Figure 58.

FIGURE 56. The painted kingfisher.

FIGURE 57. The sanded kingfisher.

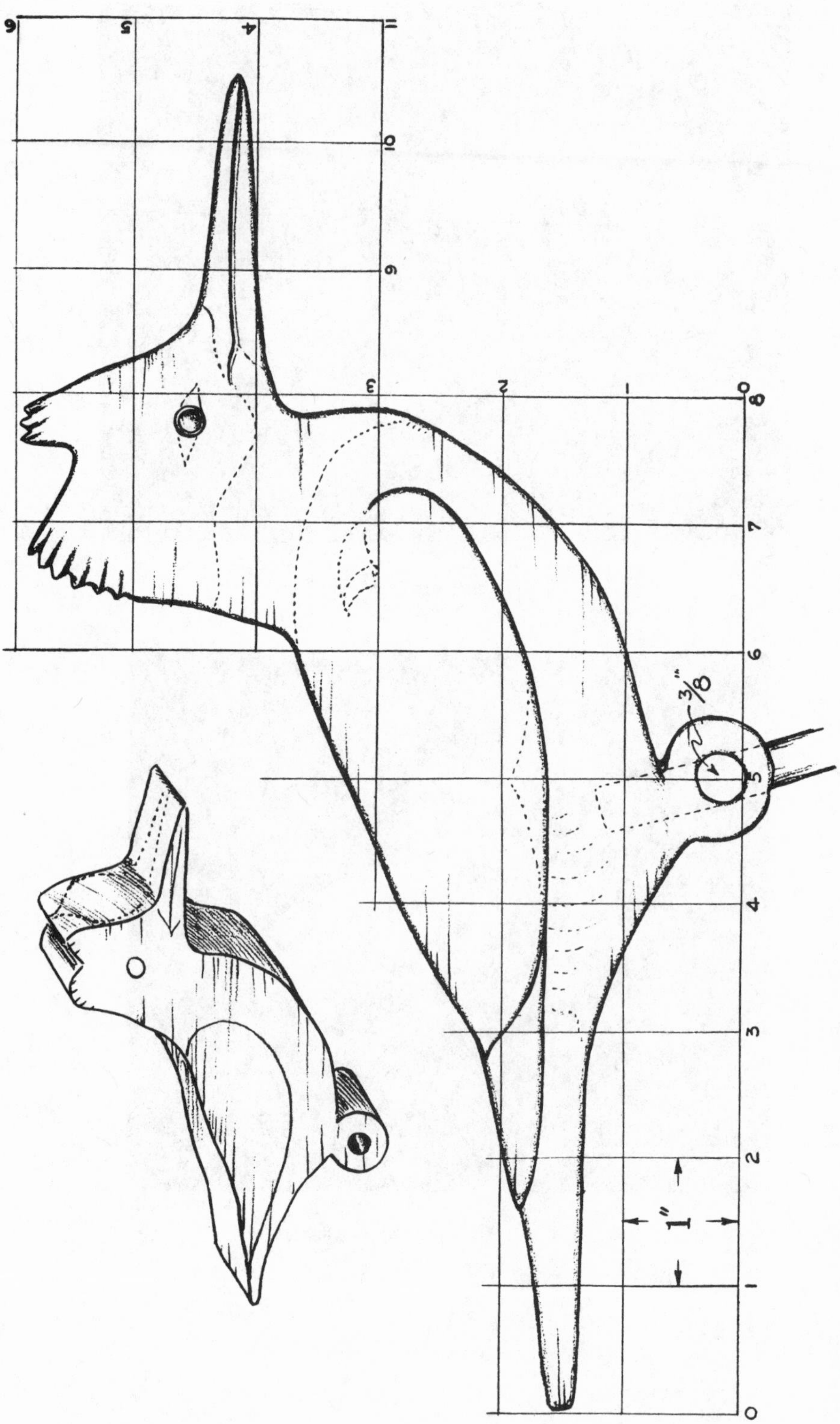

FIGURE 58.   Because of the size of this bird the pattern could not be shown full-size.   Enlarge and mark off the squares.

15 Green Cormorant

The bird shown in Figure 59 may be familiar to you. It is common in Canadian waters and is often found on the same lakes that loons frequent. (Directions for whittling the loon are found in the next chapter.) Both are fish-eating birds. The loon is black and white; the cormorant is highly colored.

When you are cutting out the silhouette, saw off the beak at the base, as shown in the inset in Figure 60 and in the left photograph of Figure 59. Then bore a $5/16$-inch hole in the head for the beak and glue in a piece of $5/16$-inch dowel rod. Whittle the beak from the dowel rod. By eliminating cross-grain in the beak, much of the danger of breakage will be avoided.

One of the qualities that give distinction to a whittling is sharp detail. Attention to details is well worth the little time it requires. A piece showing sharp detail will not easily be passed over as just another carving. As you gain skill, you will be able to carve the details that will make the project look professional. Note the beak and the feet of the cormorant. Attempt to make graceful contours. Remove all surplus wood, particularly between the feet themselves and between the feet and body. All lines should be clean-cut, especially about the feet.

The cormorant is painted in an unusual combination of colors. The beak is a greenish grey with a small section of chrome yellow on the underside near the base. A ring of brilliant vermilion is painted around the eye. The eye is white with a black pupil and a narrow black outline around the white area. The head, breast, and upper back are a brilliant green. The neck is lavender, blending into the green where the neck joins the head and where it joins the body. The lower body, back, and front are darkened somewhat with grey. The wings are a greyish green, darker than the rest of the back. The patches on the body directly above the legs are pure white. The tail is brown, and the legs are dark grey with white or light grey markings, as shown in Figure 59. For contrast, paint the base to resemble a reddish stone.

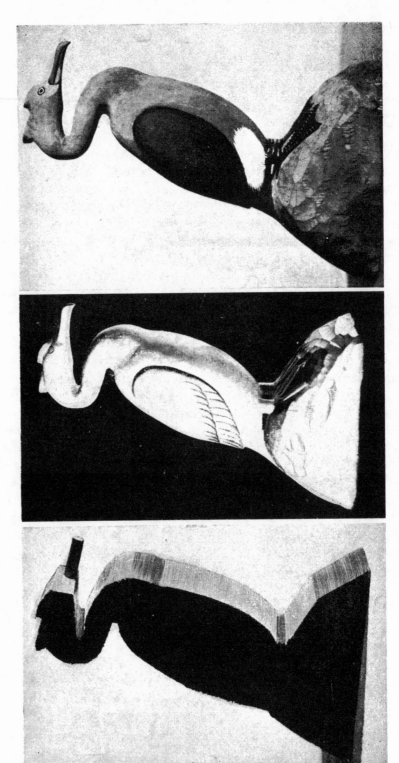

FIGURE 59. The green cormorant from silhouette to finish carving.

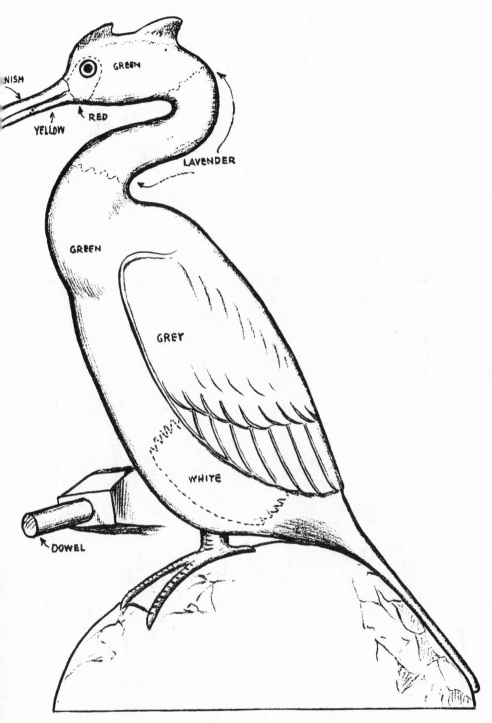

NISH

GREEN

YELLOW

RED

LAVENDER

GREEN

GREY

WHITE

DOWEL

FIGURE 60.   Side view of the cormorant.

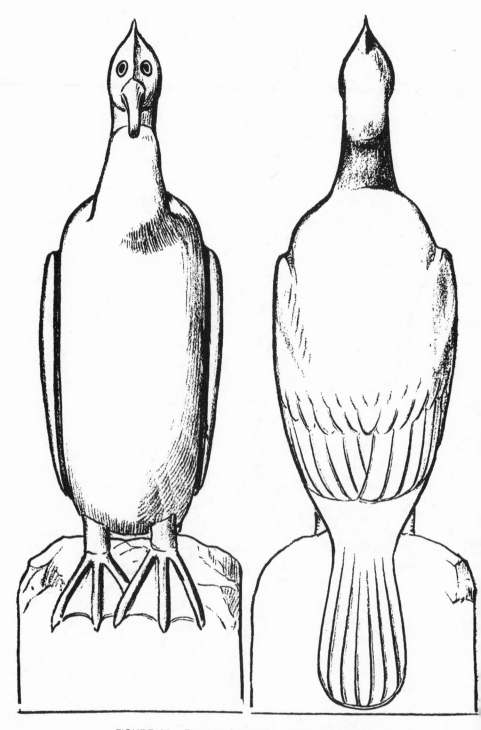

FIGURE 61.   Front and rear views of the cormorant.

16 Loon

The loon (Figures 62 and 63), with its simple marking of black and white, its long graceful body, small head, and awkward feet, is an unusual bird which is rarely viewed at close range. It is a champion diver and underwater swimmer. Its weird and lonesome call echoes and reechoes through the north woods by day and by night, but always at a distance. The spectacle of the male loon performing his mating ritual around the female, seeming to walk and dance on the surface of the water, is one which few have witnessed.

FIGURE 62. Finishing the whittling on the loon.

To whittle a loon the size shown in Figure 64, a piece of wood 2½ inches thick, 7 inches wide, and 7½ inches high is required. The extra piece for the subbase can be any piece of softwood ⅜ to ⅞ by 3 by 6½ inches. It may be glued on after the whittling is done to give the bird better stability and to prevent the regular base from chipping or splitting. The grain of the bird and base is vertical; that of the subbase is horizontal.

Draw the outline on the wood and cut it out with a band saw or a jigsaw. Cut the base of the bill as shown in Figure 64. Carefully, so as not to split the head, drill a ⁷⁄₁₆-inch or ⅜-inch hole in the center of this crosscut. Then set in a piece of dowel for the bill and secure it with glue or plastic wood. The bill should have the grain running the long way.

Perhaps the most difficult part of the whittling will be the feet and legs. A razor-sharp knife edge will be required. The wings are set quite close to

FIGURE 63.　The painted loon.

the body, being raised approximately $\frac{1}{16}$ inch.　The base can be left rough, but the body should be sanded perfectly smooth, as this bird is the last word in streamlining.　The body should not be perfectly round, but rather flattened slightly in the front and back.　Figure 62 shows two views of the loon as the whittling nears completion.

To color the bird, paint the body white and the head and neckbands black.　Then paint the markings with black paint on the white, as shown in the two views in Figure 63.　I used poster watercolors in order to avoid the gloss of oil paint, but the latter may be used if desired.　The poster colors will dry much faster than the oil paints.

The markings as shown are conventionalized, but realistic enough to avoid criticism.　Study Figure 63 carefully.　In some places, such as the sides below the wing, the black is painted over the white and the round dots are then again painted over the black with white paint.

The bill should be painted a dark grey and the eyes red with black pupils. The legs and feet are black and the base a moss green.

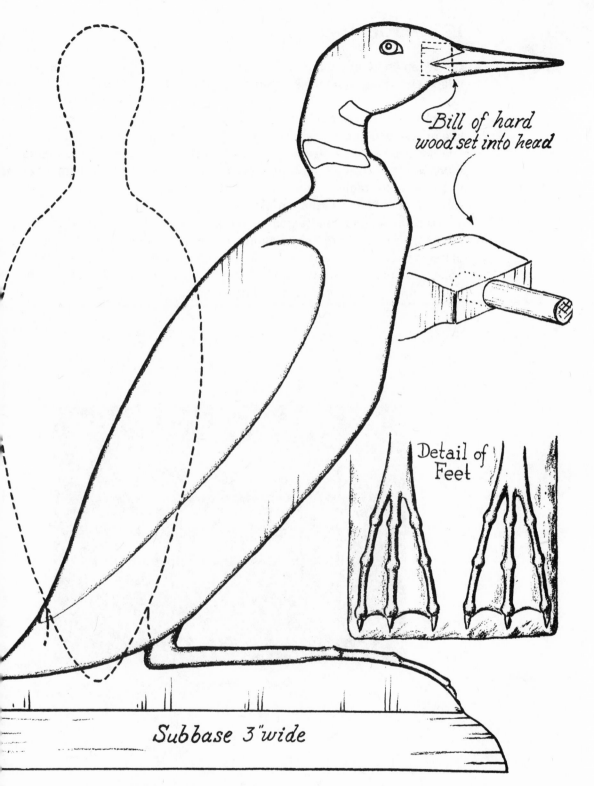

Bill of hard wood set into head

Detail of Feet

Subbase 3" wide

FIGURE 64. Full-size pattern of the loon.

17 Scarlet Ibis

When you first look at it, the scarlet ibis shown in Figure 65 seems like a difficult whittling project. Examination of Figures 66 and 67 will show, however, that it will be no more troublesome than some of the other projects. The bird shown was cut from a 1¾-inch block of sugar pine. Trace the outline on the wood and cut it out on a jigsaw as shown in Figure 66. Then outline the shape with a pencil and rough out the ibis as shown in Figure 67. When whittling the bill and the legs be careful not to break them, because they are quite fragile. The actual whittling takes less time than the jigsaw work. Figure 65 shows the bird after sanding.

The scarlet ibis may be painted a brilliant vermilion, with the feather outlines accentuated in brown and the end-wing feathers, the eyes, and the bill painted black. The legs are light brown and the base is moss green. If objects of this kind are given three or four coats of white shellac, clear lacquer, or varnish, they will look like porcelain.

FIGURE 65. The scarlet ibis.

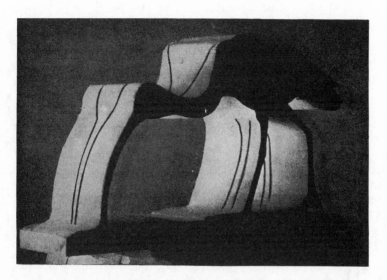

FIGURE 66. Marking off the block.

FIGURE 67. Roughing out the scarlet ibis.

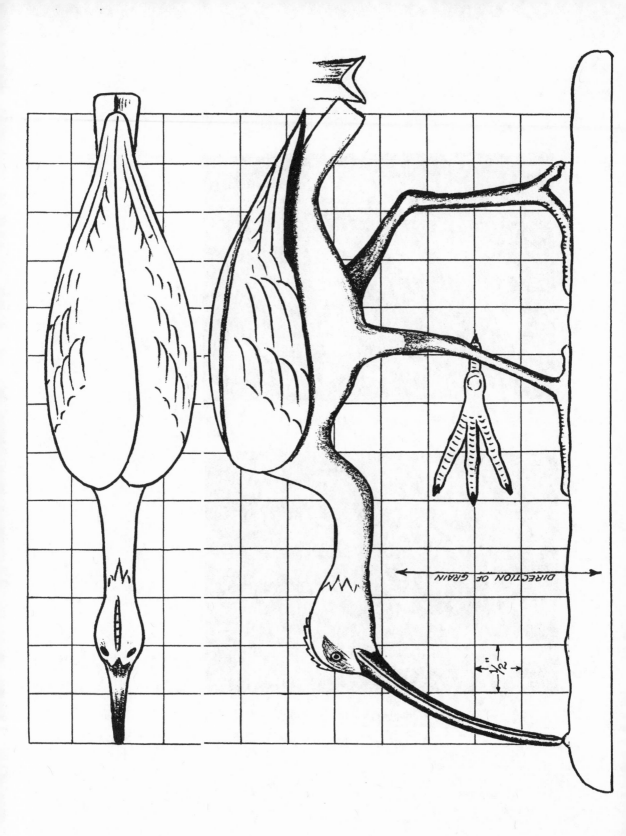

DIRECTION OF GRAIN

½"=

18 Pensive Pelican

The pelican in Figure 69 shows another type of whittling in which all the knife cuts are left visible. The whittling procedure is identical with that used on the ibis: jigsaw the silhouette, block out the project, and then do the final whittling. Figure 70 may be used as a full-size pattern. The whittling must be done carefully, however, as each knife cut tells a story.

It is a good idea to finish these whittled objects in various ways to take away the monotony that results from having all whittled articles look alike when finished. The pelican may be sanded and given several coats of egg-shell ivory enamel to make it really attractive. Or you may leave it in the raw wood. If so, finish it with either a coat of white shellac or dull varnish or several coats of liquid furniture wax or floor wax; otherwise it will become soiled very quickly from handling.

FIGURE 69. Pelican.

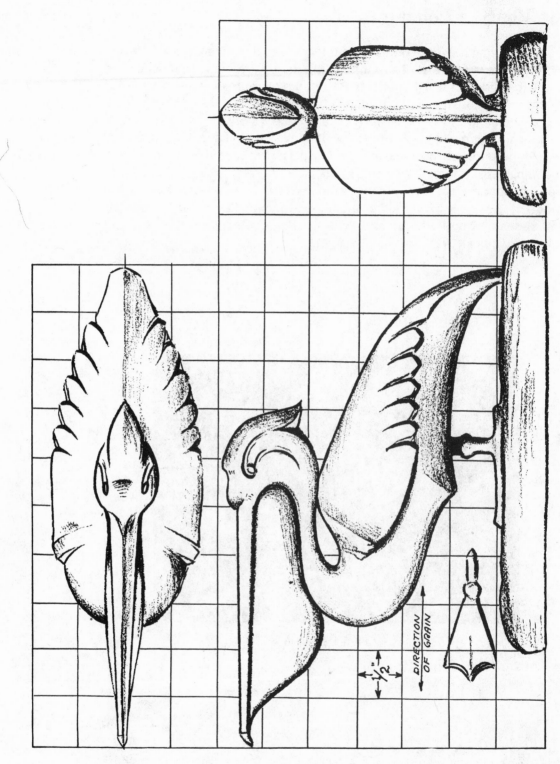

DIRECTION OF GRAIN

1/2"

FIGURE 70. Layout for the pelican.

A table ornament may be made with several pelicans used as a dish support as shown in Figure 71. The birds are whittled without the feet and are carefully sanded. The legs are then whittled out of separate pieces and set into two holes drilled in the body of the bird. Holes are also drilled into the circular wooden base. The feet are then cut into the base as shown in Figure 71. The birds and base should be finished in ivory egg-shell enamel. The bowl may be of hammered copper made to fit the base, or a wooden bowl may be turned on a lathe and painted to match the base.

FIGURE 71. Table ornament utilizing the pelican design.

Indian Crafts

19   Neckerchief Slides

Neckerchief slides make interesting whittling projects that are useful as well. The little pieces of wood required to make them can easily be carried in your pocket and whittled at during moments of leisure. Campers and scouts can work out many ideas besides the ones in these illustrations. While the designs shown in Figures 72, 75, and 77 require a little ingenuity, the whittler should not be afraid to attempt them. The wood costs practically nothing, and the results are usually satisfying. White pine or basswood is the easiest to whittle. Basswood saplings, partially seasoned, are good for this work. The whittling knife should be kept razor-sharp. This prevents slipping, insures a neat job, and enables one to do quite a bit of cross-grained and angle cutting. Most of the work on these small objects is done with the small blade of the knife.

The simplest kind of slide is the one with the incised monogram or symbol raised on its face (see Figure 72). The one shown may be whittled out of a piece of 1$\frac{1}{8}$-or 1$\frac{1}{4}$- inch sapling (when peeled), or any other softwood of the same diameter.

First rough out the block as shown in A, Figure 73. Then cut out the opening for the slide, leaving about a $\frac{1}{8}$-inch wall for the ring (see B, Figure 73). Lay out the design with a pencil and cut down about $\frac{1}{16}$ inch. Pick out the waste. Initials, monograms, symbols, and other designs may be easily whittled in this flat relief style.

It is always best to whittle out the ring first. Then if it splits—through careless handling, or because it was a bad piece of wood—not too much effort is lost. The hole in the ring need not necessarily be round. Various shapes are shown at A, B, C, and D, in Figure 74. For whittling the monogram slide, leave the front side thicker, as show in A and B, Figure 74. In

FIGURE 72. Neckerchief slide.

whittling the thunderbird and the buffalo skull, the front side is whittled thinner, as show in C and D.

Making the thunderbird or the buffalo skull will prove very interesting. The sketches of both are full-size, and measurements can be taken directly from them. Figure 76 shows the pattern for the thunderbird. This project looks more attractive if it is painted. Expression can be put in the eyes, and feathers can be painted on the breast.

The buffalo skull, shown in Figure 77, requires a larger piece of wood. A razor-edged blade is necessary to shape the horns. This slide is easier to make than it seems. The dotted lines in the side view of Figure 78 show how the inside of the skull is hollowed out. Although knife marks are fre-

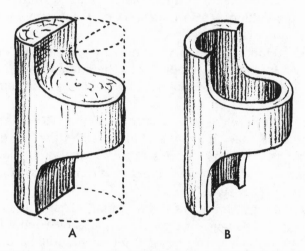

FIGURE 73. Full-size pattern and the blocking out for a neckerchief slide.

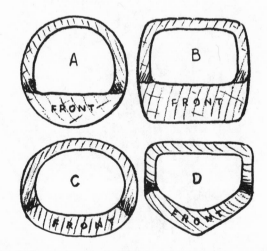

FIGURE 74. Various shapes for the hole in the ring.

quently left on some whittling jobs, there are others which it is desirable to sandpaper. This is the case with the buffalo-skull slide, which should be carefully sanded. To make it realistic, paint the horns grey or dark brown and the bone, or the skull proper, an ivory white; darken the eye sockets. Then give the whole project a coat of dull varnish. Figure 77 shows the buffalo skull before painting.

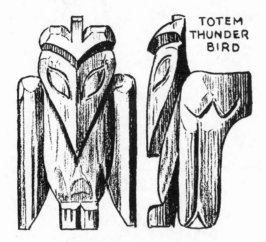

FIGURE 75. Totem thunderbird.

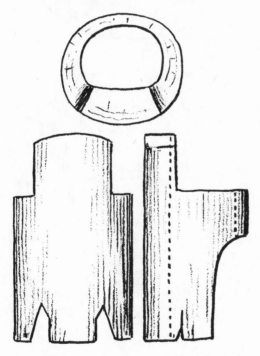

FIGURE 76. Pattern for the thunderbird.

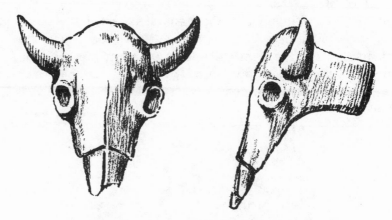

FIGURE 77.   Front and side views of the buffalo skull.

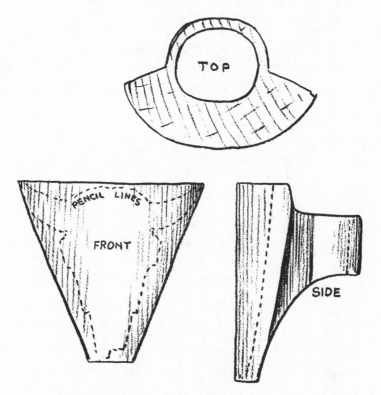

FIGURE 78.   Full-size pattern for the buffalo skull.

20 Rattlesnake and Crow's-skull Neckerchief Slides

Because of their simplicity and practicality, you may find one or both of these neckerchief slides desirable projects to make. The beginner will discover that they offer excellent preparation for some of the more difficult pieces in the book.

Crow's Skull

It is not difficult to make a neckerchief slide from a crow's skull if you have a dead crow handy. Everything considered, however, it is a lot easier to make one from a piece of white pine or basswood. For the one shown in Figure 79, it is not even necessary to saw out a silhouette, as is done for

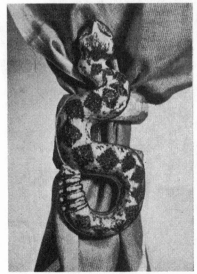
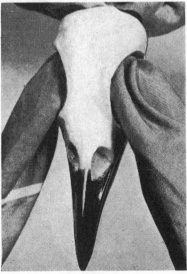

FIGURE 79. Rattlesnake and crow's-skull neckerchief slides.

most of the projects in this book. To start, whittle out the general shape, which can be taken from the top and side views in Figure 80. (Note in Figure 79 that the ends of the neckerchief cross in the skull opening and go out through the eye sockets.) This means you will have to dig out three holes. Start with the one at the top of the head; the dotted lines in the front and side views show the shape. When down almost as far as the drawings indicate, start digging out the eye sockets in the general direction of the dotted lines in the front view. When all three openings meet, complete the holes. The nostrils are formed by making oval holes straight through the beak with slightly depressed areas running toward the tip. Cut out the bottom to minimize the weight. When you have finished whittling, sand the entire skull to remove all knife marks. To paint this neckerchief slide, use Chinese white watercolor for the skull and a solid black for the beak. Paint the inside of all

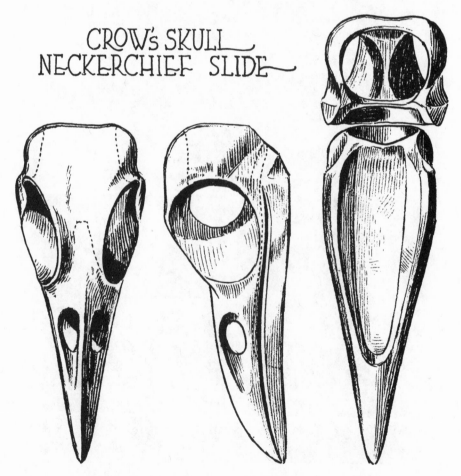

CROW's SKULL NECKERCHIEF SLIDE

FIGURE 80. Pattern for the crow's-skull neckerchief slide.

the openings a light grey for a realistic effect. When the colors have dried, apply two to four coats of clear lacquer. It takes only a few minutes for water-colors to dry. Transparent nail polish makes an excellent finish.

Rattlesnake

This unusual rattlesnake neckerchief slide (see Figure 81) also shown in Figure 79 was adapted from one that was designed by a Boy Scout executive. Many boys like snakes, and here is a chance for any boy to have a realistic rattler clinging to his neckerchief. In Figure 81, note that a section of the ring, or loop, has been cut away to make the snake stand out prominently. The original was whittled from a piece of white pine, but I have used mahogany. Instead of painting the diamond designs on the snake, you can apply them with a burning set or a red-hot wire. For the eyes, dig out small depressions just large enough for half of a small green or red bead, which should fit snugly. A drop of airplane cement or clear lacquer will hold them securely. The eyes should be set after the piece has been decorated. Several coats of clear lacquer over the snake complete the job.

The drawings in Figures 80 and 81 are full-size so that they may be used directly as patterns.

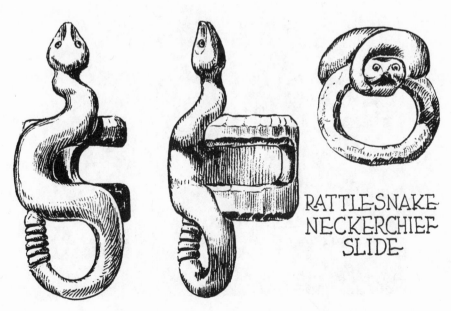

RATTLESNAKE NECKERCHIEF SLIDE

FIGURE 81.   Pattern for the rattlesnake neckerchief slide.

21 Kachina Dolls

Now let's take up some Indian lore about Kachina dolls, and then whittle a few of them. These dolls are images made to represent the mythical spirit people of the Hopi Indians, believed to inhabit San Francisco Mountain. According to the Indians, these spirits visit the pueblos at certain seasons. The Kachina dolls are made by the Hopi men and are presented to little girls at religious ceremonies. There are more than three hundred different Kachinas.

Any of the softwoods may be used for whittling these dolls. The Hopis usually used cottonwood roots, but the grain is quite rough and stringy, and they are more difficult to paint than regular softwood. Some of the original Indian dolls were dressed in buckskin or cloth skirts. However, at the present time they are decorated with paint and feathers of various colors. Four Kachina dolls are shown in Figure 82, complete with watercolors and feathers. Figure 84 shows three Kachina dolls ready for painting.

Figure 85 shows the way the wood is marked off, the saw cut for the legs, and the finished whittling of one type of doll. No faces are whittled, as most of the Kachina dancers, whom the dolls represent, wore masks. The ornamental top panels at the side of the masks are glued into mortises, or slots (see Figure 86). The noses shown in Figure 87 are set into mortises in the same manner. Figure 90 shows that not all masks have noses and that there are several characteristic masks of the more ornamental type. Notice how

FIGURE 82. All painted up!

the features are represented by using symbolic figures and just a few lines. Some of the dolls are decorated with feathers, others are not.

Three styles of legs and two different kinds of feet are shown in Figure 91. The legs in the upper left-hand corner are whittled without the saw cut. Also note that one of the dolls in Figures 82 and 84 has a different kind of mask and no arms. It is supposed to be wearing a blanket. Any of the masks may be used on any of the bodies, and the same holds true of the feet and legs. These Kachina dolls do not necessarily follow every detail of the original Indian dolls but are intended to be pleasing to the eye. The nicest proportion for these dolls is $1\frac{1}{4}$ to $1\frac{1}{2}$ inch in diameter by $3\frac{1}{2}$ to 5 inches high. These dimensions may be changed to suit individual tastes. Some of them are made as large as 3 inches in diameter and 12 inches high. The legs, too, may be made longer or shorter, as may the skirt. Study the key to the colors shown in Figure 90. If you have the opportunity, look at Kachina dolls in a museum. Figure 83 explains the meanings of some Pueblo symbols used in decorating these dolls.

These interesting little figures are well worth the time it takes to make them. Even children can whittle them, and at camps they make fine handicraft projects which can be produced at little cost. A few ten-cent jars of poster colors will decorate quite a few dolls, and feathers are easy to come by. Only small feathers should be used.

Some of you may want to go further and whittle a Kachina dancing doll. The drawings in Figures 88 and 89 illustrate how to whittle the dolls to show action. The arms are fastened on with a small brad and glue, and the rattles and other articles may be added. These can be made in groups for table-top decoration, showing almost any one of the dances of the Hopi or Zuni. These dolls are not of Indian origin, but just a thought on my part for something a little different.

FIGURE 83. Indian symbols.

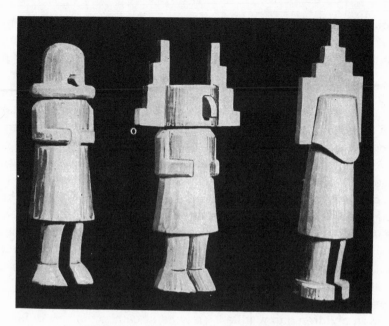

FIGURE 84.   Ready for the paint and feathers.

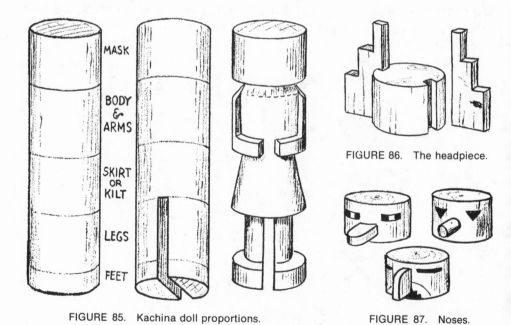

FIGURE 85.   Kachina doll proportions.

MASK

BODY
&
ARMS

SKIRT
OR
KILT

LEGS

FEET

FIGURE 86.   The headpiece.

FIGURE 87.   Noses.

FIGURE 88. Kachina dolls showing action.

FIGURE 89. Kachina dancing doll and table lamp.

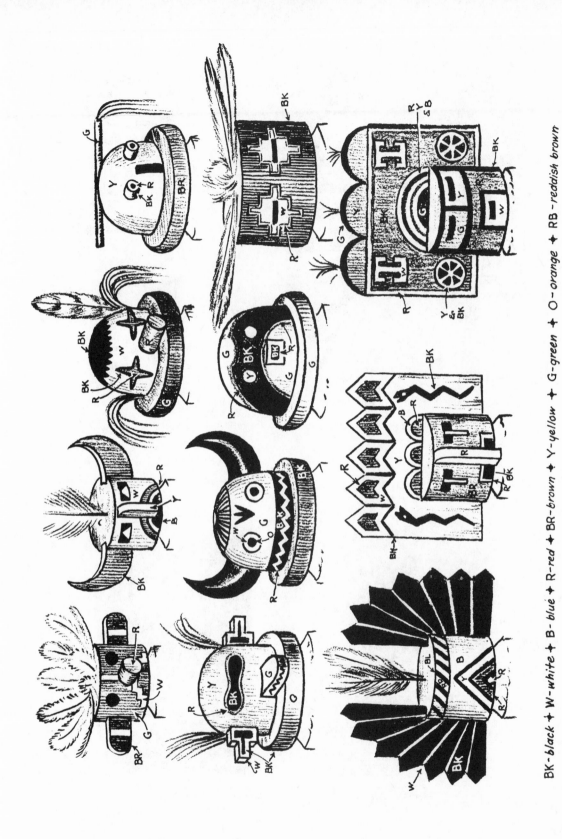

FIGURE 90. Designs and directions for painting Kachina doll masks.

BK - *black* ✦ W - *white* ✦ B - *blue* ✦ R - *red* ✦ BR - *brown* ✦ Y - *yellow* ✦ G - *green* ✦ O - *orange* ✦ RB - *reddish brown*

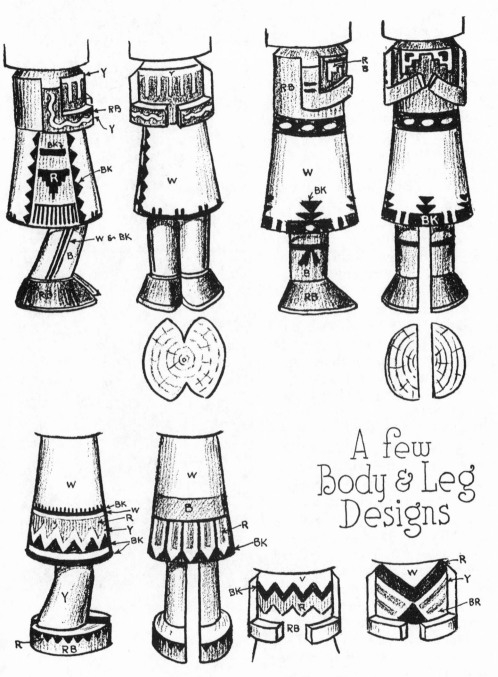

A few
Body & Leg
Designs

FIGURE 91. For color key see Figure 90.

22 Totem Poles

Totem poles are interesting to most people because almost everyone is acquainted with these peculiar carvings which our northwest Indians place in front of their houses. Each totem pole tells a story, or is symbolic of the family who owns it. They are usually carved out of huge cedar logs with axes, chisels, and adzes.

The ornamental totem poles shown here are only 12 and 13½ inches high. This is a handy size for whittling. They may be made of any size, however, from ornamental pins 2 or 3 inches high to full-sized totem poles 10 or 20 feet high. The ornamental totem poles may be made from a square of wood rounded off on the front, or from a softwood sapling flattened off in the back as shown in Figure 93.

The two poles shown in Figures 94 and 95 consist of several units. The totem pole shown in Figure 94 is symbolic of the raven and the wolf. These ornamental poles can be painted if desired. White, black, red, brown, blue, green, and yellow are the colors ordinarily used, but much of the beauty of the whittling is lost when it is covered with paint. If the poles are simply tinted a brownish grey resembling the color of old, weathered totems, they will appear realistic, and the whittling will show up better. A square or round base may be nailed to the bottom of the totems to make them more stable.

Lay out the largest units or parts

FIGURE 92. Totem poles.

with a pencil and start by roughing out each one. Then draw the details with the pencil. The shading has been omitted in the drawings to avoid confusion. Study the illustrations in Figure 92 to get the various planes, as they were left unpainted for this purpose.

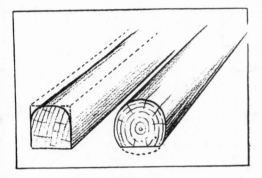

FIGURE 93.

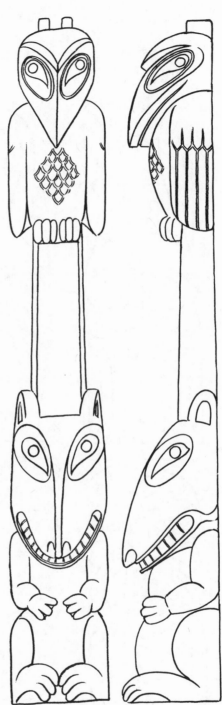

FIGURE 94. The raven and the wolf totem pole.

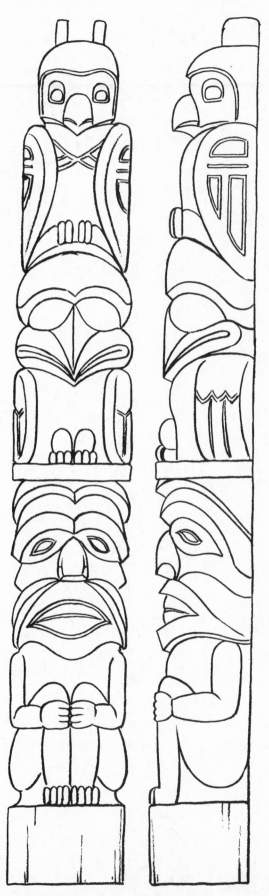

FIGURE 95.   A miniature totem pole.

23 Indian-head Neckerchief Slide

More difficult than those I discussed earlier is the Indian-head neckerchief slide shown in Figures 96, 97, and 98. This slide is very ornamental when painted. In whittling faces like these, study the drawings carefully be-

FIGURE 96. Indian-head neckerchief slide.

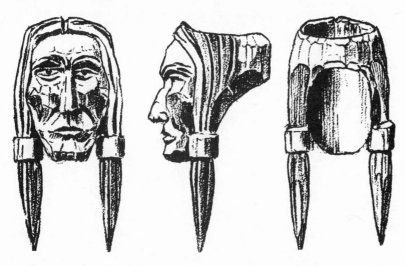

FIGURE 97. How to carve the Indian-head neckerchief slide.

FIGURE 98. Indian-head neckerchief slide before painting.

fore cutting, especially after the rough cutting and forming is done. Even the simplest face is rather tricky, as every cut tells a story. So whittle slowly, study the drawings, and study each cut until you know what it will mean in the finished work.

This neckerchief slide should be painted with watercolors: the face an Indian red, the lips a brighter red, the eyes black, the hair black, and the hairband yellow. Give the face a thin coat of shellac and the hair several coats, to give it a glossy appearance. Leave the inside of the slide unfinished and slightly rough to prevent it from slipping.

The Indian head may also be used as a lapel ornament, in which case the back should be left flat.

24 Canoe in the Rapids

This project, and the three that follow, will introduce most whittlers to a more advanced stage of handicraft. You will be making not only a figure but a setting for it as well. This involves assembling several different pieces of whittling to complete the whole. There is nothing absolutely new, however, and if you have learned to whittle the simpler projects, you will be able to do this one.

The canoe in the rapids shown in Figure 99 was made out of four pieces

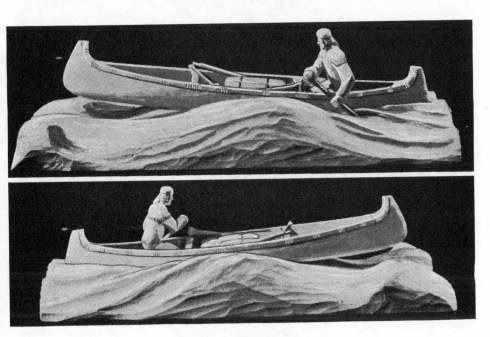

FIGURE 99. Canoe in rapids.

of wood which were glued together as shown in Figure 101. A one-inch board was used for the base. Before the gluing is done, the canoe should be sawed to shape at both ends. Figure 101 shows how it is to be cut. The shape of the canoe can be traced from Figure 100. The two ends of the canoe that project beyond the small blocks at the sides should be whittled to shape before the pieces are assembled. When the glue has dried, rough out the waves and the outside of the canoe. Then the inside can be gouged out. Do not try to carve out the inside of the canoe before gluing the sections together. It may seem to be the easier way, but since the glued joins should be as inconspicuous as possible, pressure will have to be applied to force the edges together, and this cannot be done after the canoe has been hollowed out. A crooked knife was used to whittle the waves and to hollow out the canoe. The thwarts, or seats, were glued in later (see Figure 102). The

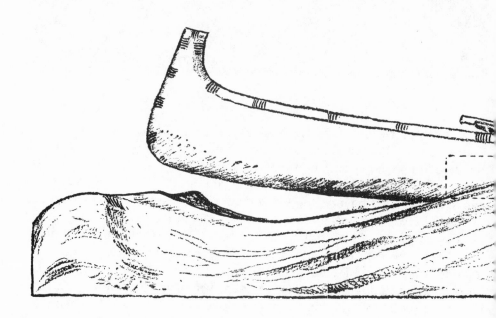

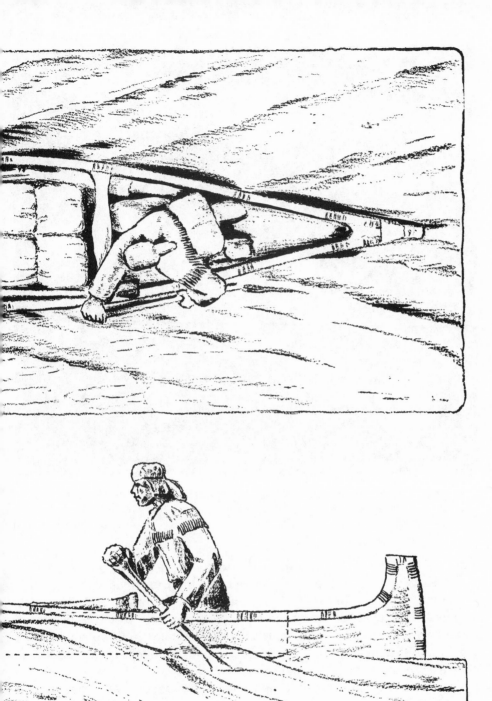

FIGURE 100. Top and side views of the canoe in the rapids.

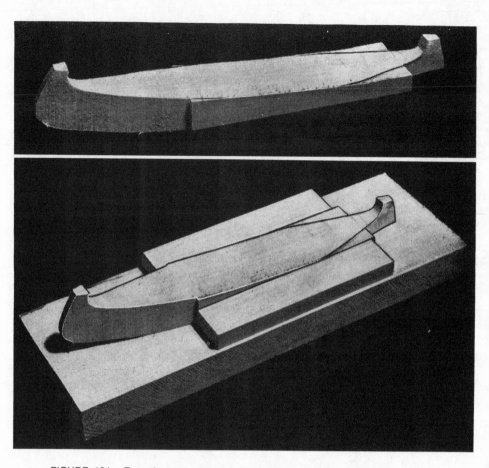

FIGURE 101. Top, the canoe sawed out; bottom, the pieces glued into place.

gunwale, or strip around the edge of the canoe, is slightly wider than the canoe walls and the wrapping is simply indicated with small V cuts.

The trapper is more difficult to whittle than the canoe and the waves, because to show action he has to be considerably off center. However, if you follow closely the different views shown in Figure 102, you will have no great trouble in making him. The bundle in this figure represents a rolled-up blanket. To the right of it is the handle of the paddle. The trapper's hands are hollowed out to fit the grip and shaft. The paddle will probably give you a little trouble, but by whittling off a slice here and there it can be made to fit in snugly. It actually snaps in place and holds the trapper in position. The larger package, shown in the canoe in Figure 100, represents a bundle of furs. It is not among the items shown in the details in Figure 102, but it can easily be made. If you care to load the canoe with additional duffle of your choosing, go right ahead.

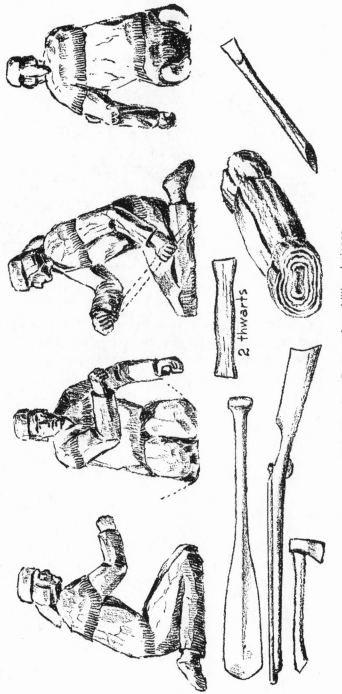

FIGURE 102. Patterns for additional pieces.

2 thwarts

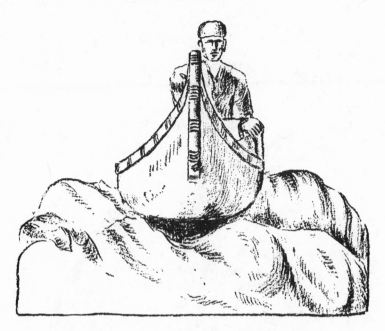

FIGURE 103.   Front view of the canoe in the rapids.

The finish is a matter of choice. If all the wood is from the same piece of lumber and has the same color, it may be well to leave it as is, including the knife cuts.   The finished piece can also be sanded and painted in suitable colors.

25 Indian Head

The Indian head shown in Figures 104 and 105 was made out of mahogany. Cherry, walnut, pine, or basswood also might have been used.

Start out as usual with the silhouette of the side view (see Figure 106).

FIGURE 104.   The Indian head after painting.

When you are ready to whittle the face, set up a mirror so that you can see your own face. Then, too, you might look at another person and study his face as you proceed with the whittling. In this way you will see a lot of things that cannot be shown in drawings or photographs.

If the feather should break off, it is a simple matter to glue or cement another one onto the back of the head. The headband represents a beaded band such as the Blackfoot Indians wear. The hair is shown wrapped with cloth instead of being braided, but where there is no wrapping it is lined with fine V cuts which follow the natural sweep of the hair. The neck beads were made with a small hollow nail set. A bear-claw necklace might have been used and would also have been effective.

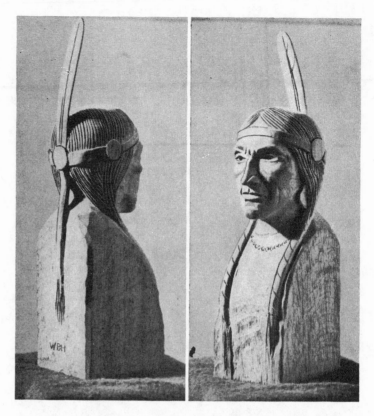

FIGURE 105. The Indian head after whittling.

Whether the project is to be painted or not is a question that must be decided by the individual whittler. Some who saw this head said they would have liked it unpainted. Others have said it looks much better painted. Well, this is a matter of opinion. Your friends will consider it an attractive piece, painted or unpainted.

To finish the Indian head without paint, first give it a coat of filler to close up the pores if it is mahogany. Then it can be stained dark and waxed.

If cherry or walnut is used, all you need to do is to give the piece one or two thin coats of linseed oil, and after the oil is dry, wax it.

If you decide to paint the head, start with the hair. Apply a coat of black watercolor or waterproof drawing ink. The headband then is painted white, and after that the designs are put on in red, blue, black, and orange. The hair wrappings are a bright red and the shell ear pendants are white. The eagle feather is white with a black tip. The face can be given a coat of dark mahogany stain, or it may be painted with reddish brown watercolor. The rest of the block can be left natural, as shown in Figure 105.

FIGURE 106.   Front, left-side, and rear views of the Indian head.

26 Indian Travois

The travois was a vehicle of the Indians of the Great Plains. As shown in Figure 107, it consisted of two trailing poles with a platform or net for the load. The travois is a favorite subect of artists. Here is an opportunity for you to make one. You will note that this project has been left in the rough state—that is, the knife cuts have not been removed. If the cuts are rather uniform, the effect is very pleasing. White pine was used for the horse and squaw and for the tepee bundle on the travois. The travois and the three crosspieces are of willow—which, by the way, had to be stained to match the pine. (Willow is whiter than pine.) The Indian woman is a Sioux with her blanket wrapped around her. Her leggings show below the edges of the blanket.

This project is whittled from more than one piece, and then assembled. You will probably wonder why the horse and Indian were not whittled separately. The two were made out of one piece because this is a lot simpler than trying to fit the squaw snugly on the pony. Holes are drilled along the pony's sides, under the squaw's thighs, for the travois, as shown in Figures 108 and 109. A small hole is also drilled through the mouth of the pony for the rope, and the other end of the rope is then inserted into a hole in the squaw, so that she appears to be holding the rope and blanket at the same time.

To assemble the project, cut a piece of rough orange-crate wood about 4 by 15 inches. Glue or cement the pony in place first. Then attach the travois poles, which must be cemented and pegged to the base. Tie these in place to dry. While the poles are drying you can attach the crosspieces by cutting small notches on the undersides, and fastening them to the poles with a drop of cement. Allow the cement to dry and tie the crosspieces at each side. The bundle is then fitted to the crosspieces, set in place with a few dabs of cement, and lashed. For a finish, you can apply a few coats of clear lacquer to everything but the base.

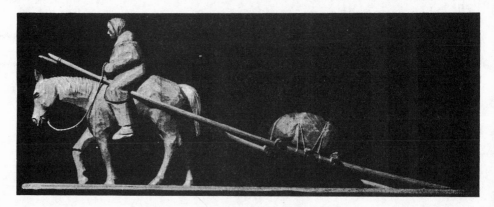

FIGURE 107. The travois on the move.

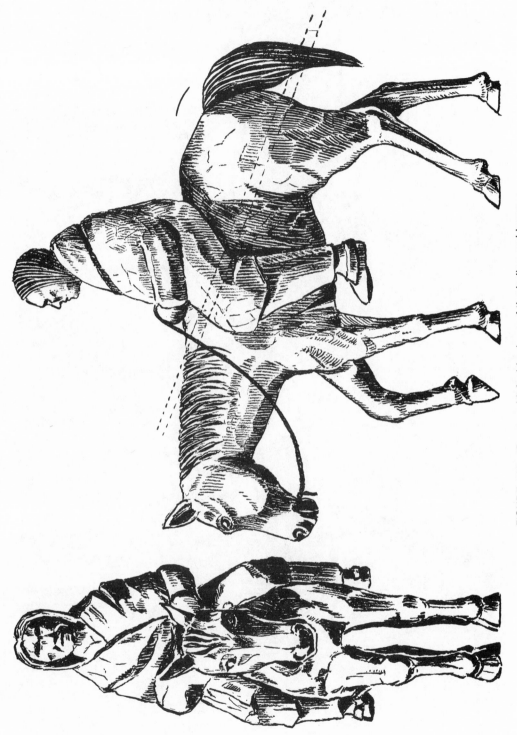

FIGURE 108. Front and left-side views of the Indian and horse.

FIGURE 109. Rear and right-side views of the Indian and horse.

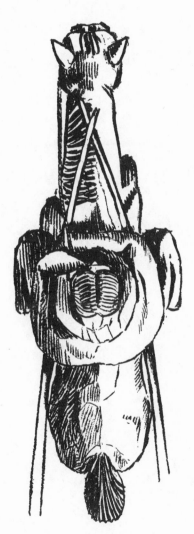

FIGURE 110. Top view of the Indian
and horse.

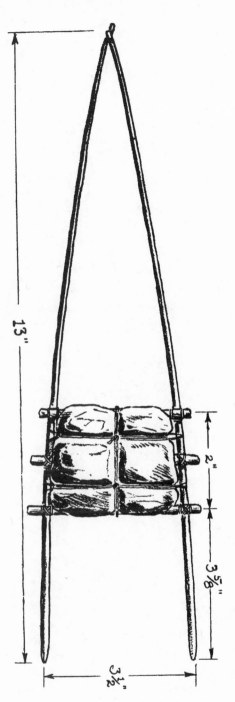

FIGURE 111. Patterns for the travois
and load.

Animals in Wood

27 Norwegian Pigs

The whittled animals in this section of the book are quite different from one another in kind and in the qualities which each suggests. The zebra colt looks spry, and the moose powerful. Some of the animals are stylized, like the buffalo, and others are true-to-life, like the seal. Many have been included in response to repeated requests from whittlers—for example, the horse. I think you will not only find these pieces desirable to have around but will also have a lot of fun making them.

Who said "pigs is pigs"? Who would want to put a pig in the parlor? Scrub that pig to a pure white, however, place a wreath of roses around her neck and a pretty embroidered blanket on her back, add a few other spots of color, and you have a pig that is a pig, one to whom you will gladly give a place on the mantel shelf (see Figure 112). You may even want to make room for a few little pigs besides. To make such a group is very simple. A couple of evenings, and you will have them all whittled, painted, and lacquered. Some persons believe that whittled pigs of this particular type are of Norwegian origin. Whatever the case, they make a pleasing and unusual ornament.

FIGURE 112. Norwegian pigs.

After you have cut the silhouettes and whittled the pigs, you can paint them as they are, if the knife cuts were carefully made, or you can sandpaper them if you prefer. Give each pig a coat of white watercolor. The blanket is cream or light buff as shown in Figure 113. The outer scallops are red, fading out as shown, with a black edging and dots. The floral design is red, black, and green. The oval spots on the sides and back are a very light blue with a cream center outline with black dots. The wreath around the neck consists of red circles for the roses and two green stems connecting them. Eyes, mouth, and hoofs are black. The pigs should be given a couple of coats of colorless lacquer.

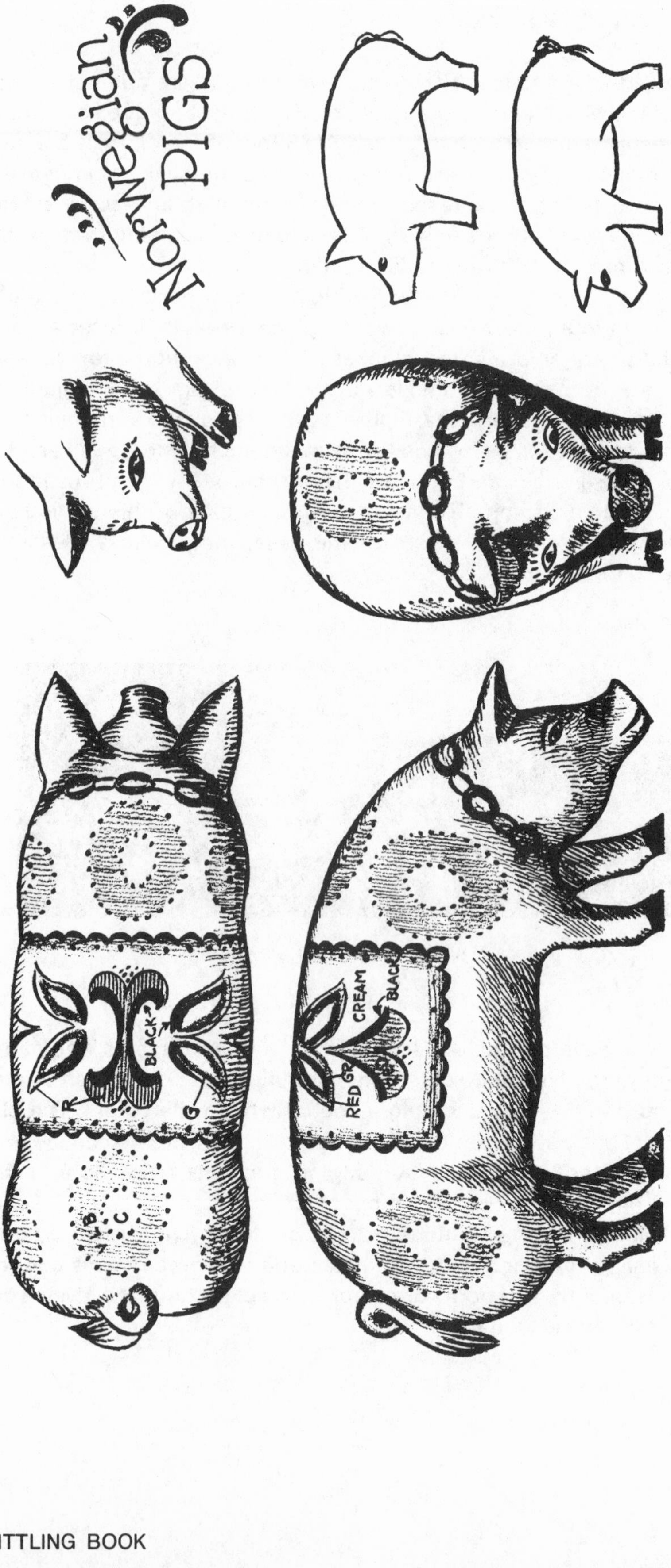

FIGURE 113. Patterns for the Norwegian pigs.

28 Seal

This seal is really streamlined. That means that the whittled seal calls for some fine sandpapering. However, there are a few things that must be done first. Cut out the silhouette from a 3- by 4¾- by 5¼-inch block of wood. The seal shown in Figure 114 was whittled out of mahogany, but any softwood will do. The grain runs up and down.

FIGURE 114. Seal waxed and polished.

After the block has been cut, lay out the top view as shown in Figure 117. Note that the seal is not exactly centered on the base. The front, side, and rear views are shown in Figures 115, 116. A crooked knife will save a lot of time in roughing out the seal. The finished whittling is not too difficult, as every part is more or less rounded.

After finishing the whittling, smooth the seal with fine sandpaper, being careful not to sand the base. The seal may then be given a coat of brown walnut stain. After wiping it carefully, let it dry; then two coats of floor wax should be applied. As a last touch polish it with a soft cloth.

If the seal is whittled of mahogany the same procedure should be followed. Use the thick stain from the bottom of the can because it will act as a filler to close or fill the pores that are so noticeable in mahogany. Figure 114 shows the seal after waxing and polishing.

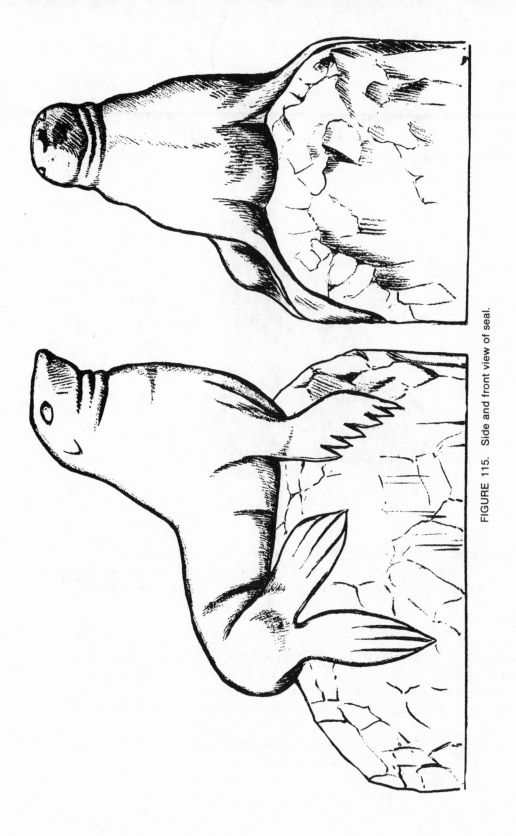

FIGURE 115. Side and front view of seal.

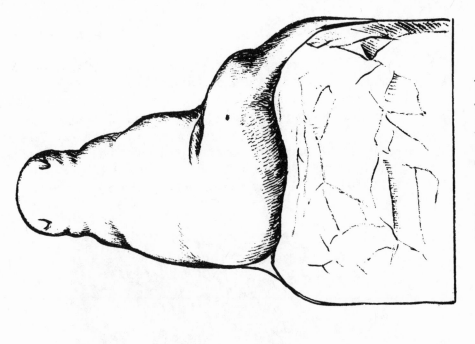

FIGURE 116. Rear view of seal.

FIGURE 117. Top view of seal.

29   Zebra Colt

The little zebra colt shown in Figure 119 presents a rather simple job of whittling. With the grain running up and down, the legs are not hard to shape. Four full views are given in Figure 120. After the silhouette is sawed out, pencil in the legs and then block out the entire figure; that is, shape every part of it in square areas instead of rough, round areas. This procedure makes it easy to obtain the correct proportions. The rounding up and finishing is rather simple, and the final finishing is, of course, done with sandpaper. Figure 118 shows the zebra colt whittled and sanded.

FIGURE 118.   The zebra colt whittled and sanded.

Give the entire figure a coat of Chinese white watercolor and let it dry. If you are not too sure of yourself, pencil in some of the stripes before painting. You need not be too concerned about the exactness of the stripes since no two zebras are marked exactly alike (see Figure 119). For the striping, use a good black watercolor and mix it so that it is not too thin. Notice that the stripes meet down the center of the back and belly. As you paint a stripe on one side, paint a corresponding stripe on the other side. The final finish should be a coat or two of clear lacquer. Shellac and varnish have a tendency to yellow the white somewhat, and though the real zebra may not have pure white stripes, pure white and good solid black look better on this piece.

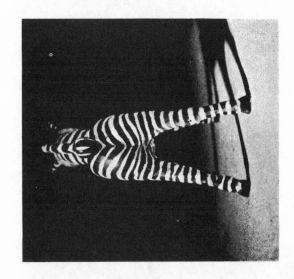

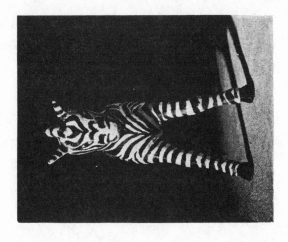

FIGURE 119. Front, side, and rear views of the zebra colt showing how it is painted.

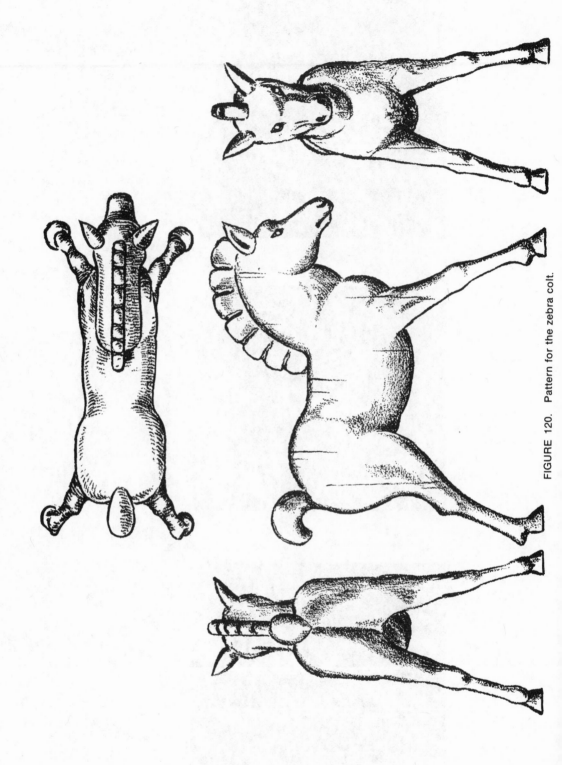

FIGURE 120. Pattern for the zebra colt.

30　Buffalo

This whittling project is a very simple, modernized version of the American buffalo. The one shown in Figure 121 was made out of mahogany. Other kinds of wood, such as walnut or pine, can be used and the results will be equally good. Mahogany is classed as a hardwood, but in reality it is as easy to whittle as pine. Probably the only difficulty it presents is that wood filler must be used to obtain a smooth finish.

FIGURE 121. Buffalo.

Bear in mind that the crooked knife is excellent for roughing out—you can rough out an object in just about half the time, and with half the effort, as when the work is done with an ordinary pocketknife. After the rough work has been done, a pocketknife is used to finish the job. On some of the jobs, even the finishing can be done by making small cuts with a razor-sharp crooked knife.

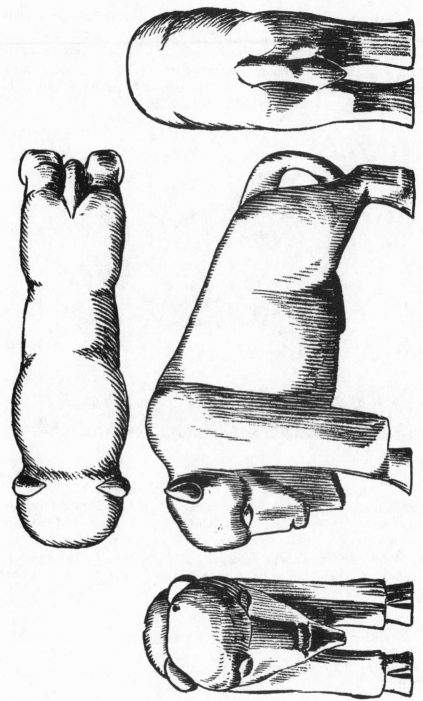

FIGURE 122. Pattern for the buffalo.

31   Grizzly Bear

The grizzly bear presents a real problem to the whittler. It may look simple to whittle, but it requires quite a bit of undercutting, which makes it rather difficult. Figure 126 and Figure 127 show views from which to work. Study them, and figure carefully before you begin to whittle. Since the grain runs up and down, most of the cutting will be across it. This means that the knife must be razor-sharp. A small, crooked knife will come in handy on this job. To carve the bear you may use soft white pine, cottonwood, or poplar.

To start, draw or trace one of the side views onto the block of wood and cut out the silhouette on a bandsaw or jigsaw. Then bore the holes between the legs as shown in Figure 124. The next step is to block out the legs and head as shown in Figure 125. If these simple directions are followed, it will be a lot easier than trying to whittle out the rounded shape from the start. After the legs are separated and the head squared in, start the rounding-up process gradually. A long, thin-bladed knife will be found best for cutting beneath the body and around the legs.

After you have whittled out the grizzly, the next question is how to finish it. You might leave clean knife cuts rather than to try to make the grizzly's hide look like fur. When the bear looks just about as you want it, go over the whole figure again with a razor-edged knife, making small, clean cuts. Then sandpaper the face and ears a little, just to smooth them. Do not sand the entire bear, or it will look as if it were skinned.

The whole bear may now be colored with a yellowish brown stain or watercolor (see Figure 123). The base may be colored grey. Do not use oil stain, as the predominance of end grain will make it too dark.

FIGURE 123. The finished grizzly.

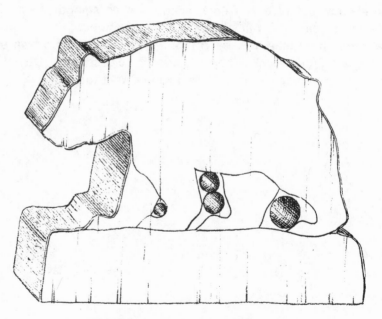

FIGURE 124. Cutting out the silhouette.

FIGURE 125. Blocking out the head and legs.

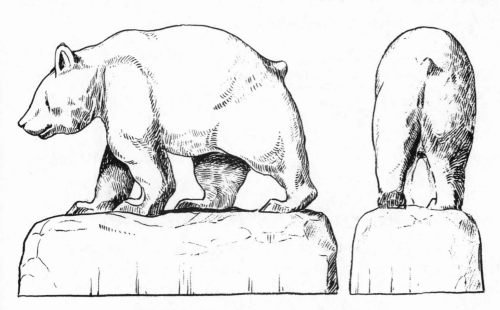

FIGURE 126A. Side and back views of the grizzly bear.

FIGURE 126B.   Side and front views of the grizzly bear.   Illustrations may be used as half-size patterns.

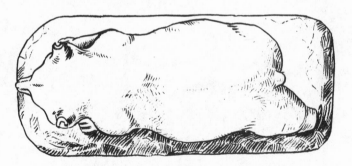

FIGURE 127.   Top view of the grizzly bear.

32 Howling Wolf

A piece of wood 1¾ by 4⅜ inches, with the grain running up and down, is required for whittling out the wolf shown in Figures 128, 129, and 130. This one was whittled out of a piece of mahogany, but any of the softwoods will do equally well.

Draw the outline on the block and cut out the silhouette in the usual manner. Notice that the tail projects ½ inch from the left side of the wolf. Before starting to rough out the figure, cut ½ inch in from the left side of the wolf, letting the part for the tail stand. Then start blocking or roughing out. No base has been left on this piece, which makes the lower part much easier to whittle. The ruff, or hair around the neck, and the tail have been made quite simple. The figure has been left with the knife cuts showing. You may sand the wolf, but it looks better if the knife cuts show; then the figure will have a more rugged appearance, which is in keeping for an animal of this kind.

As far as the finishing goes, the wood may either be left in its natural state or given a few coats of wax to prevent soiling. A glossy finish would not be very appropriate for this wolf.

FIGURE 128. Howling wolf.

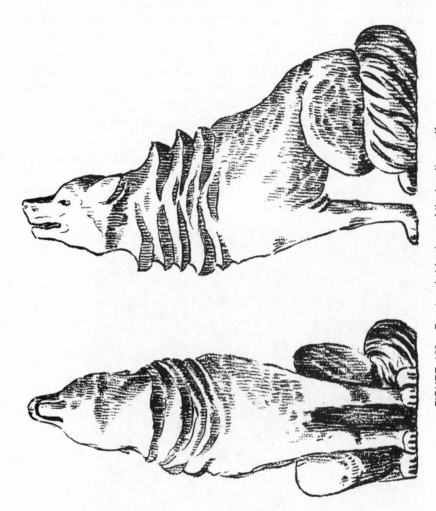

FIGURE 129. Front and side views of the howling wolf.

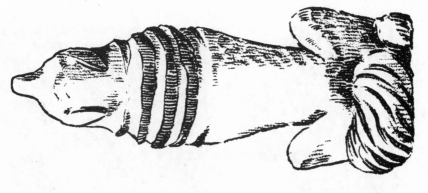

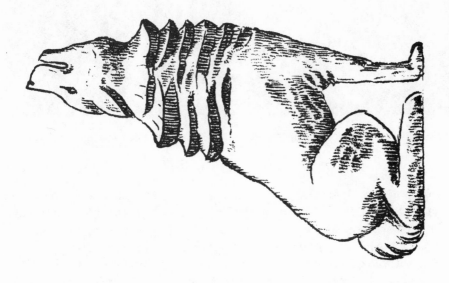

FIGURE 130. Rear and side views of the howling wolf.

33   A Rearing Horse

At first glance, whittling the horse shown in Figure 132 might seem extremely difficult.   This is not the case, however, and after the silhouette has been prepared and the animal blocked out, the job will look a lot easier.

FIGURE 131.   The silhouette of the rearing horse.

FIGURE 132.   Rearing horse.

Probably the most difficult parts to carve are the back legs and the tail. The tail is attached to the base, as shown, in order to make it less breakable. But this is not absolutely necessary, especially if walnut or mahogany is used, since the horse is so carved that the grain runs up and down.

The author carved this horse from a block of mahogany.   For this piece, mahogany can be finished beautifully with either mahogany or walnut stain. If Honduras mahogany is used, the body can be given a light coat of walnut stain and the mane and tail left natural.   This will make it look like a palomino pony.   The photograph for Figure 132 was taken before staining.   Walnut oil stain was then applied.   After the stain dried, the statuette was waxed and polished, and it now has the appearance of old bronze.

FIGURE 133. Side view of the rearing horse.

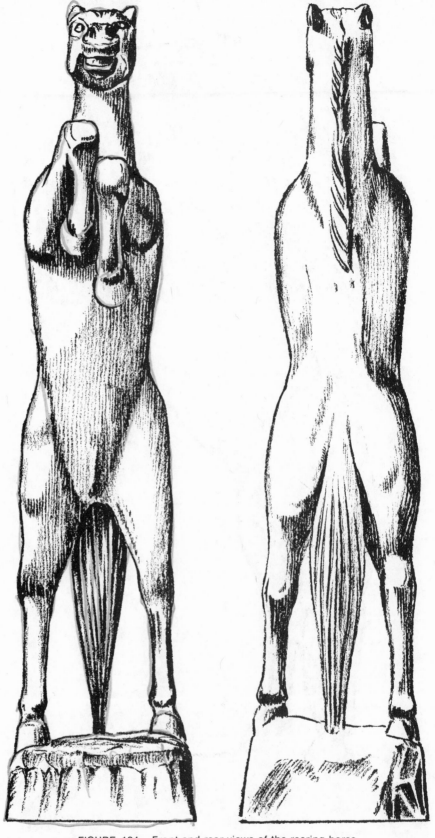

FIGURE 134.   Front and rear views of the rearing horse.

34 Bull Moose

The bull moose shown in Figure 135 offers a challenge to those who really like to whittle. The body will not be difficult if you select a good piece of wood. I used mahogany. It is, as I have already said, an excellent wood to work with. Moreover, the color cannot be surpassed for a project of this type. The grain can run either horizontally or vertically. If the grain runs horizontally, the whittling of the body proper will be easier. The legs in this case will be cross-grained. If the grain runs vertically, the legs will be easier to whittle, but the body will present more work.

I suppose that you have been wondering about the antlers. They will be a test of your whittling ability for two reasons. First, they are somewhat delicate. Second, they must match. The antlers will require skill no matter how you go about them. In making the model, two methods were experimented with and both were successful. However, the simpler method will be explained in detail.

FIGURE 135. Bull moose.

Prepare a block using the pattern shown at *A* in Figure 141. Cut out the template at *B* and lay out the two antlers on the block, reversing the pattern for the left antler. Then cut out the silhouettes with a band saw or jigsaw. Next shape the concave surface at *C*, and after that, the convex surface. Rounding the prongs is tedious rather than difficult inasmuch as you are working with cross-grain at the tips. Be sure that your knife is razor-sharp.

Here is another method for making the antlers. Lay out the side and front views of the antlers on a block (see Figures 136 and 138). On the top in-

FIGURE 136. Left-side view of the moose.

dicate the alignment of the prongs (see Figure 140). Saw out the silhouettes (side view) and whittle the antlers.

I would like to call two points to your attention. First, a crooked knife will be found very helpful for forming the curved surfaces of the antlers. Second, you may find it easier to get the two antlers to match if you whittle them simultaneously.

After the body and antlers are whittled, the latter are fastened to the

FIGURE 137. Right-side view of the moose.

FIGURE 138. Front view of the moose.

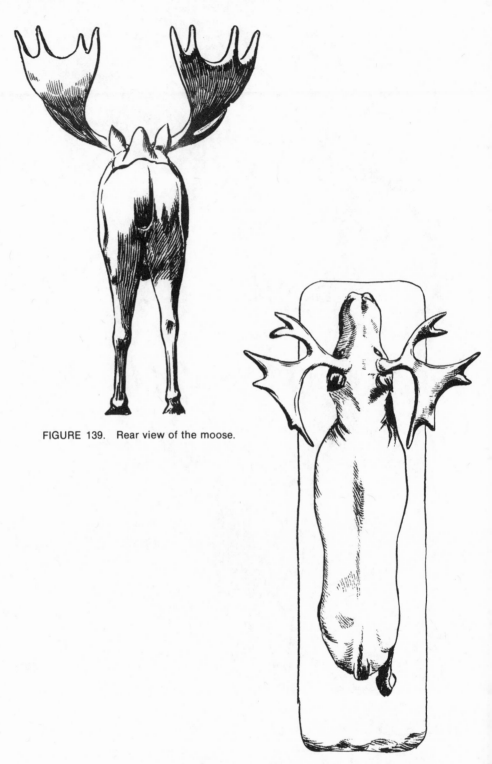

FIGURE 139.   Rear view of the moose.

FIGURE 140.   Top view of the moose.

head. There are two methods. First determine the slant of the antlers and cut a flat surface on the skull for them to rest on. Then cut *round* tenons on the butt of the antlers as shown at *D* in Figure 141, and cut *round* mortises

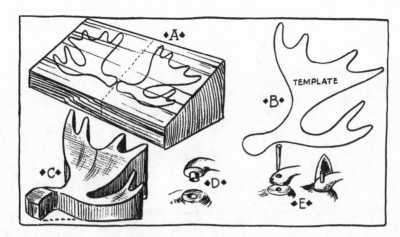

FIGURE 141. Details for cutting out and mounting the antlers.

into which they fit. It is important that the mortises and tenons be round because after the cement has been applied and the antlers set in place, you may have to twist them in order to get them straight. Use either airplane cement or any one of the common, fast-drying household cements. They set in a few minutes and harden overnight.

The other method of fastening the antlers is to use pegs, as shown at *E* in Figure 141. First determine the slant of the antlers, cut the flat surfaces on the skull, and then cut the butts of the antlers to correspond with these surfaces. Now you will need either four hands or a helper, because the antlers must be held in place while the hole is drilled through the base of the antlers into the skull. Use a $\frac{1}{16}$-inch drill. Then whittle two slightly tapered dowels long enough to project about $\frac{1}{4}$ inch above the base of the antlers when they are set in place. After the dowels have been fitted and the antlers balanced, remove the dowels, put a drop of cement on each one, and set them into the bases of the antlers. Then put more cement on the bottom of the pegs and the butts and press the antlers in position. If the dowels fit and the antlers are in proper position, set the job aside until the cement is dry. If the fit is not snug, tie the antlers, making use of the projecting ends of the pins to keep the thread from slipping. When the cement has hardened, cut off the projecting ends of the dowels and sand carefully. If the antlers do not fit perfectly, fill the openings with glue, dust the glue with wood dust, and allow it to dry. The wood dust is made by filing a piece of the wood out of which the moose was made. A little trimming and sanding will do the rest.

35 Sailfish

Trace the side view of the sailfish, as shown in Figure 144, onto a piece of wood, being careful to have the grain running in the same direction as the beak, which is rather thin.   If desired, the beak and the back fin, or sail, can be set into the fish by drilling a hole for the beak and a slot or groove for the

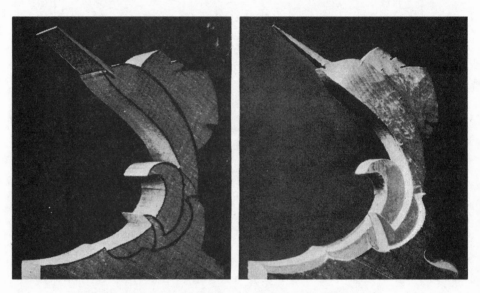

FIGURE 142.   The silhouette and blockout of the sailfish.

FIGURE 143.   The sanded and finished sailfish.

fin. The one shown was whittled out of one piece. After cutting out the silhouette (Figure 142), draw a center line down the back of the fish, because it is not centered, but swings to one side at the tail end. Then block out the fish and waves as shown. While the beak must be whittled thin, the large fin may be made almost ¼ inch thick at the base. It tapers toward the outer edge and the front and rear, and the thickness of the base is not noticeable. The large fin requires the most work. After shaping, make V cuts as shown in the drawing. Photographs of sailfish show us that no two *sails* are alike, so one need not be too fussy. The other side of the fin can be left smooth.

Carving the fish is not as difficult as carving the waves. For the waves a crooked knife should be used.

Everything can then be carefully sanded. Figure 143, left, shows the sanded sailfish. It may be left at this stage or it can be stained and varnished, or it can be painted with watercolors, as shown. If you can get a colored picture of a sailfish, it will make the painting much easier. The back of this fish is a dark Prussian blue, almost black, which gets lighter as it goes down the sides. Then there is a white streak followed by a light blue streak. The light blue is made by mixing white with the Prussian blue. The light spots along the upper sides are also light blue. The eyes are orange with black pupils and the mouth and edges of the gills are a deep pink. The lower fins are tinted with pink and a touch of yellow. The large fin is a medium blue with white streaks and black edges. The belly is white with a streak of light grey down the center. The tail is black. Paint the water a sort of lettuce green with bluish shading and white streaks here and there to look like foam. When the watercolors have dried, give the entire piece about four coats of lacquer (clear fingernail polish).

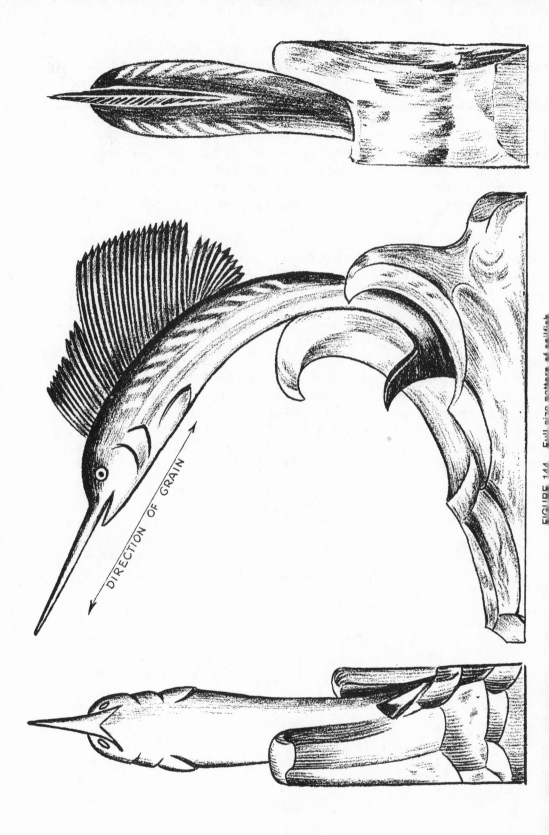

DIRECTION OF GRAIN

FIGURE 144 — Full size patterns of swordfish.

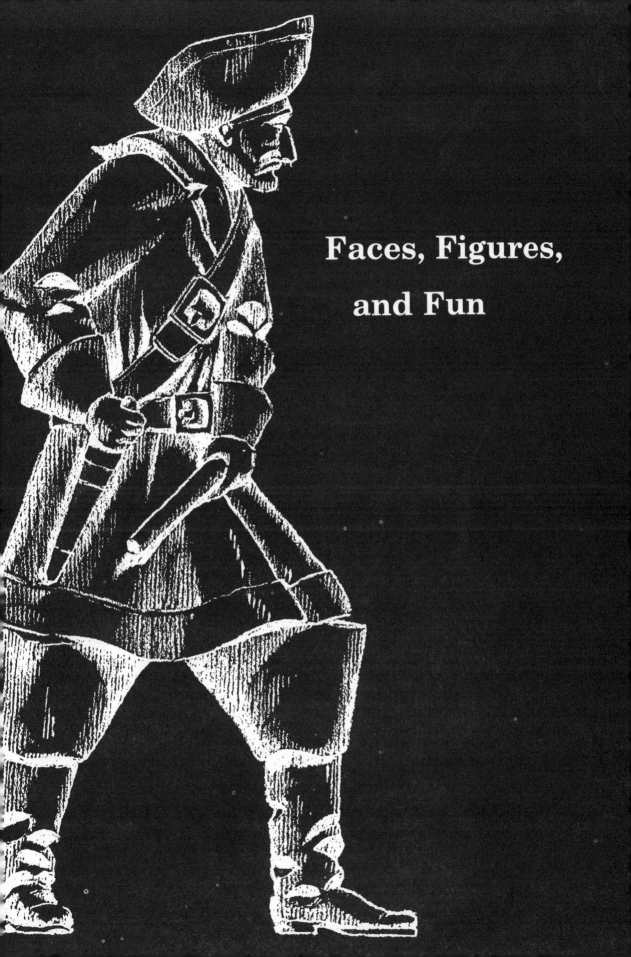

Faces, Figures,
and Fun

36 Ethiopian Boy's Head

After whittling birds, animals, totems, and Kachinas, it is only natural that we should try our hand at whittling the face and figure. Never forget the human interest element when you select whittling projects. Some people might not be too enthusiastic over this or that bird or animal, but most people will express interest in a human figure that is worth its weight in wood.

At some time or other, every whittler has the urge to try to whittle a head. The little fellow shown in Figure 145 may be a good project to start with since the whittling is not too difficult. No attempt was made to get the texture of his short curly hair; only the hairline is shown.

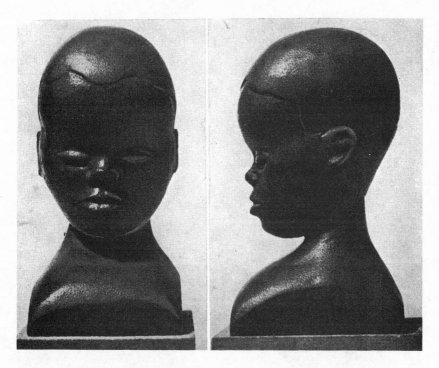

FIGURE 145. Front and side views of the Ethiopian boy.

This was a very absorbing piece of work. I completed the job in two hours, including the staining. It was waxed the next morning when the stain had dried. The head was whittled out of a piece of mahogany $1\frac{7}{8}$ by $2\frac{1}{8}$ by $3\frac{5}{8}$ inches.

Cut out the side silhouette shown in Figure 146. This should be done very carefully. You will appreciate the exactness of the sawing after you start whittling. It is advisable to saw just up to the outline, letting the line stand. In this way you can be certain that there will be sufficient wood to

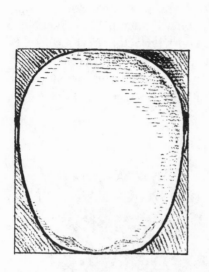
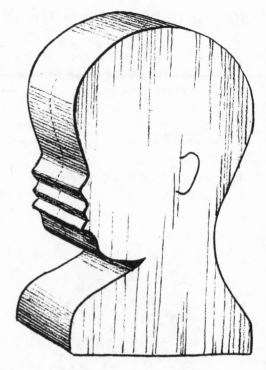

FIGURE 146.   The silhouette.

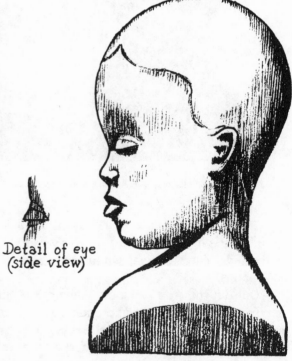

Detail of eye
(side view)

FIGURE 147.   Full-size pattern for the Ethiopian boy.

form the nose and lips. The ears should be traced and drawn on each side, because they come out to the edge of the block, as shown in Figure 147.

Before you start to whittle, draw a center line down the front of the silhouette and indicate the position of the eyes, and the width of the nose and lips. Then study Figures 146 and 147. Note the top view.

Begin by forming the top of the head and work downward.

To finish the Ethiopian boy's head, first apply a coat of filler, then give it a coat of brown walnut stain. After this has dried, wax it to bring out the highlights.

37 A Little Fisherman

The project shown in Figure 148 consists of three whittled pieces: the boy, the dog, and the fish. They were made of basswood. The grain should run up and down for both boy and dog. This project could have been whittled

FIGURE 148.   Little fisherman.

in one piece, but it is much simpler to make each piece separately. The boy and the dog are fastened to the base by drilling a small hole in the right foot of the boy and the left front foot of the dog and then setting them on a small brad driven up through the base from below. This is shown in Figure 149. A drop of glue or cement on each of the feet, the dog's and the boy's, will secure them.

The fish pole, which should bend to show the weight of the fish, is made of a thin strip of bamboo. To shape the pole, heat the bamboo over a candle or gas flame and bend it with your fingers. It will bend very easily, but care must be taken not to let it catch fire while it is being heated. The butt of the pole is then cemented to the hand, which is whittled to fit it. Any white thread can be used for the fishline. Perhaps you would like a larger string of fish; if so, whittle on.

This particular project has been left natural to show it off better. If you want to paint it, use thin, transparent watercolors. Paint the trousers light blue to resemble washed-out overalls, the shirt yellow, and the hat a straw

FIGURE 149.   Right and front views of the little fisherman.

color.   The face, hands, and feet should be a good suntan color, and the dog black or brown.   Since it is rather difficult to whittle the eyes, they can be drawn in with watercolor with a few simple lines, or a dot of dark color can be used.   The fish can be painted grey and green with a white belly.   The base can be either painted green or colored to suggest sand.

FIGURE 150.   Left and rear views of the little fisherman.

FIGURE 151. Pattern for the fish.

FIGURE 152. Pattern for the dog.

38 "Houn' Dawg"

Every now and then one sees whittled caricatures of animals that are amusing and refreshing departures from the usual type of work which tries to copy nature more or less closely. These caricatures permit much freedom of design and are, therefore, great fun to whittle. You can proceed boldly without worrying about the outcome. Most of us are not cartoonists, but we can nevertheless get many ideas from cartoons in magazines and books, which may be copied or adapted as whittling projects.

FIGURE 153. Right- and left-side views of the "houn' dawg."

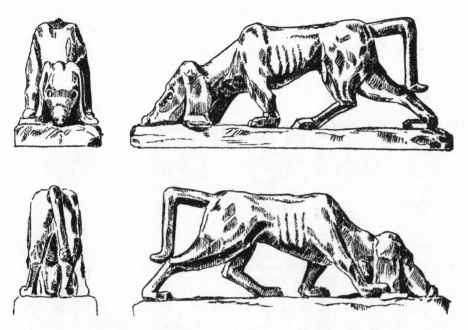

FIGURE 154. Make the "houn' dawg" larger than shown.

Caricatures—or cartoons, if you care to call them that—will be interesting no matter how grotesque and impossible they are when whittled. Very likely you would not want a "houn' dawg" like the one shown in Figure 153 running around the house, but this particular specimen will look very well on a table in the den, or on the whatnot shelf in the living room, and it will attract attention.

Not much need be said about whittling this dog. The grain of the wood runs horizontally. The dog's features can be exaggerated even more than they are here, if desired. For instance, he might be made thinner or heavier, or other changes can be made to suit your liking. No matter what you do, you can be quite certain that you will have a funny-looking pooch when you have finished.

The problem of coloring can be left to the judgment of the whittler. However, white with liver-colored spots will be found effective. You can let the natural color of the wood take the place of the white and use brown for the spots.

39 A Buccaneer

This tough-looking buccaneer (Figure 155) may look like a difficult job of whittling, but it is not as hard as it looks. After the silhouette has been sawed out, it may be well to start at the hat, and work down to the belt line.

FIGURE 155. The buccaneer roughly whittled, sanded, and painted.

Then lay out the soles of the boots on the bottom and work back to the waist-line. Keep the whittling quite rough at the start, and do not cut away too much wood. Be careful to allow for the pistol and the belts. The belts are whittled after the rest of the figure has been finished.

There are two ways to go about whittling. One is to reproduce objects in exact detail. The other is to present an approximate reproduction. Both have their place. For the buccaneer, the latter procedure was followed, and it proved very satisfactory. Try to achieve action and balance, and do not be too much concerned about getting your article to look exactly like the one shown. After all, no two buccaneers looked exactly alike. If you do not care for the type of boot I used, make loose pantaloons above the top of the boot, ommiting the flare from the boots. Then, too, you may prefer a wide-rimmed hat with a flat crown.

If the figure is whittled out of cherry or mahogany, it need only be sanded

FIGURE 156. Right-side and front views of the buccaneer.

and waxed and you will have an excellent finish. If it is whittled out of pine or basswood, you will probably want to paint it. The buccaneer is colored as follows: The hat is dark green with the upper edge a deep yellow. The face and hands are a reddish brown, with eyes, eyebrows, wisps of hair, and mustache black. The cloak is bright vermilion with collar, cuffs, and lower hem deep blue. The boots are black. The belt and sash are russet leather color, and the buckles are old gold to suggest brass. The pistol is grey, and the dagger sheath is dark brown with brass trim.

The base was omitted to facilitate whittling. The figure of the buccaneer can be glued to any type of base you choose. You could make a pair of buccaneer bookends without too much difficulty. Of course, two figures would be required. They could be mounted on a 1-inch board rounded at the front with the corners of the uprights left square. You could paint each of them different colors for variety.

FIGURE 157.   Left-side and rear views of the buccaneer.

40 Mountaineer Moonshiner

The old, white-whiskered mountaineer moonshiner trudging up the mountain lane with a keg of his product on his back makes a very interesting whittling job. As shown in Figures 158 and 159, the old man has a frown on his face which makes you feel as if he wished the whittler would hurry so that he could set down his keg and take a rest.

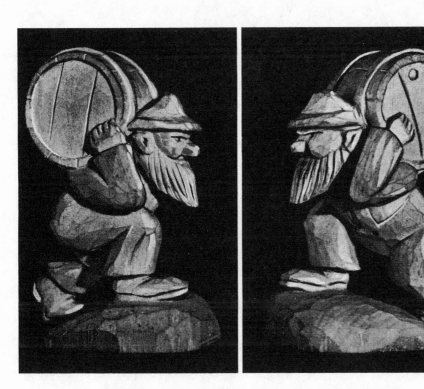

FIGURE 158. Right- and left-side views of the mountaineer.

To start, cut out the silhouette. If you do not saw out the opening between his legs, bore a few holes to facilitate the cutting out of this section later. Start whittling at the top. Determine the width of the keg and cut away the sides, being careful to leave wood for the hands. After this has been roughed out, do the legs and arms, leaving the face for the last. This procedure is suggested because a slip of the knife in the earlier stages will not harm the face when it is still in the rough. Then, too, if the face is done last, you will have the feel of it better than if you had whittled it first.

The rough whittling shown in the illustrations is what the southeastern mountain people call chip carving. Possibly you prefer a smooth finish.

FIGURE 159. Pattern for the mountaineer.

However, for such a rugged individual as this mountaineer seems to be, chip carving is much more effective. Do not attempt to duplicate too closely the knife cuts in the drawings and photographs. Simply proceed in your own way and try to make each cut count. The keg is roughly whittled to look like a real keg. The ends are set in and the hoops stand out. The hoops are exaggerated, but that adds to the general effect.

Color the keg a brownish grey with black or darker hoops. The mountaineer's hat is light brown, the shirt yellow, the suspenders red; the trousers are blue with patches painted on one side of the seat and on the right knee. The stitches should be white, so that the patches will look as if they were sewed on with string. The shoes are brown with lighter color on the sides and toes to simulate wear. The face and hands are pink, the cheeks and nose red, and the whiskers white. A narrow white streak for eyebrows will make the old mountaineer look rather angry. The eyes are merely black spots. The base is brownish green. The colors suggested can be varied according to your preferences.

41 Big Bad Wolf

There is no denying the fact that the big bad wolf shown in Figure 160 is rather a sorry-looking critter, but he is not as tough as he looks. That is, he is not hard to whittle, because you cannot make him look worse than he is depicted here. If you can improve on his *bad* looks, I would like to see a photograph of your version.

FIGURE 160. The surly, slinking, big bad wolf.

This job is not difficult and consequently requires little comment. However, if this is one of your first jobs, don't make the mistake that many beginners make—not cutting away enough wood. Don't hesitate to whittle your pieces down to size. If a piece is too thick, get your knife razor-sharp and go over the entire surface if it needs it. There is little danger that you will spoil it, and it is more than probable that it will have better lines than before. Try this on the wolf if necessary, and do not sand the finished job. You have

FIGURE 161. Front and left-side views of the wolf.

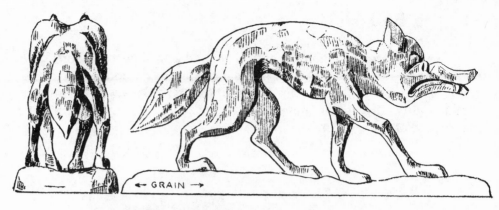

FIGURE 162.   Rear and right-side views of the wolf.

FIGURE 163.   Top view of the wolf.

most likely noticed that the perspiration from your hands will soil a nice white whittling job.   This is unavoidable, because it is necessary to grip the piece firmly, and that makes your hands perspire.   Using an eraser on the wood will not remove the stains.   By going over the entire figure with a sharp knife you can clean up the carving and at the same time thin down the object.

42 "Drizzly Bear"

And here is another one of those awful-looking critters (see Figure 164). Personally, I can't see why anyone would want to own a character like this, much less go to the trouble of making him. I whittled only two of them, one homelier than the other, and then I started to get nightmares.

FIGURE 164. "Drizzly bear."

Once the silhouette is sawed out (see Figure 165), it takes only a short time to whittle this caricature of a bear. It will not even be necessary to saw out the midsection. Just drill a few holes, and since the legs on both sides are alike, the silhouette will be completed with a few cuts of the knife. Removing the wood between the hind legs at the haunches will be a bit tedious. However, by cutting with the tip of the knife through the opening between the front legs, you will be able to remove the surplus wood.

This figure can be made even more humorous if it is painted. Start at the nose with a light brown and add a little more brown for the body as you proceed. Leave the underpart lighter. Then darken up the ears a bit, paint the nose black, and make the lips and the rims of the eyes a bright red. Paint the eyeballs cream or white and draw a short black line across them. The photo was made from one that was not painted.

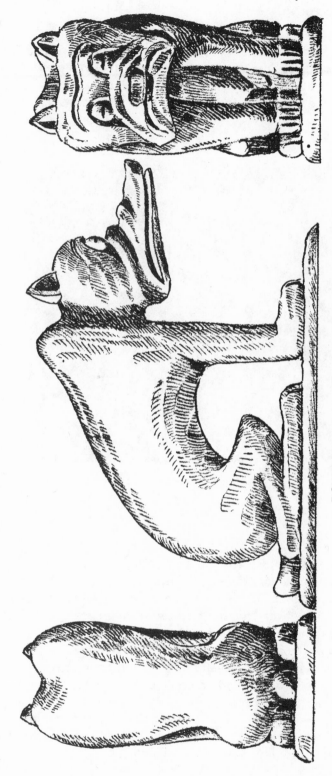

FIGURE 165.   Pattern for the "drizzly bear."

43 Mexican Oxcart

This Mexican oxcart is a beautiful project when finished. It involves a combination of whittling and model making. The several pieces are whittled and constructed separately and then assembled to form the oxcart.

FIGURE 166. Mexican oxcart.

The ox leans slightly to the left with its right front foot raised. Trace the ox as you see it in Figures 167 and 168, but when you are selecting the block of wood, be sure it is at least 1¾ inches thick to allow for swinging the head to one side. You may have trouble balancing the ox on three feet, but if you trim off the two left hoofs a bit, it will balance as shown in the front view of Figure 167. The entire project is chip carved, or rough carved. If the whittler prefers, the ox may be sanded, but the rough texture is in keeping with the object.

The cart should be made according to the measurements given in Figure 170. The long poles, or shafts, and the two round crosspieces are made of willow shoots, but any wood will do. After all the pieces are whittled, fasten the shafts and plank to the axle with airplane cement and, when dry, fasten the two end crosspieces to fit up against the bottom of the plank. After the cement has hardened, it is an easy matter to drill small holes in the shafts for the stakes and also for the wooden pegs that hold down the plank. The plank should show knife marks to represent adz cuts.

Lay out the wheels with a compass, drill the holes, and cut around the rim with a band saw or jigsaw. Then whittle them as shown. The little Mexican boy and the pulque jug shown in Figure 169 are easy to whittle. The bow of the yoke can be made of a piece of rattan like that used for weaving baskets. You may have to bend it to fit the ox's neck—or you can cut out a little

FIGURE 167. Top, right-side, and front views of the ox.

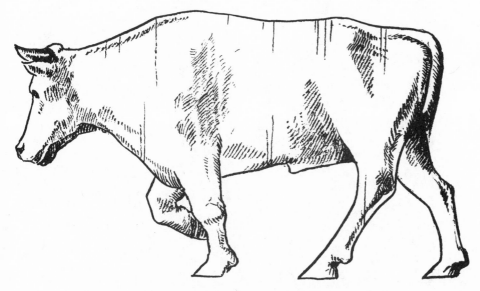

FIGURE 168.   Left-side view of the ox.

FIGURE 169.   Patterns for the boy, pulque jug, and yoke.

of the neck to fit the bow. If you cut the neck, try to make it look as though the bow is pressing into it. The spring of the bow is sufficient to keep it in place in the upper part of the yoke.

If the Mexican oxcart is to be painted or lacquered, this is done before the project is assembled. When finished, it is mounted on a base.

There are various things with which you can load the cart. The cart in Figure 166 is loaded with sticks whittled from scrap wood and also small branches and twigs with the bark trimmed off. These sticks are white. The project as a whole thus has a white appearance which is very interesting. A small groove is cut into the seat of the boy's pants, and his stick for driving the ox is placed in this groove so that it appears as though he were sitting on it. Everything except the load of wood should be glued in place.

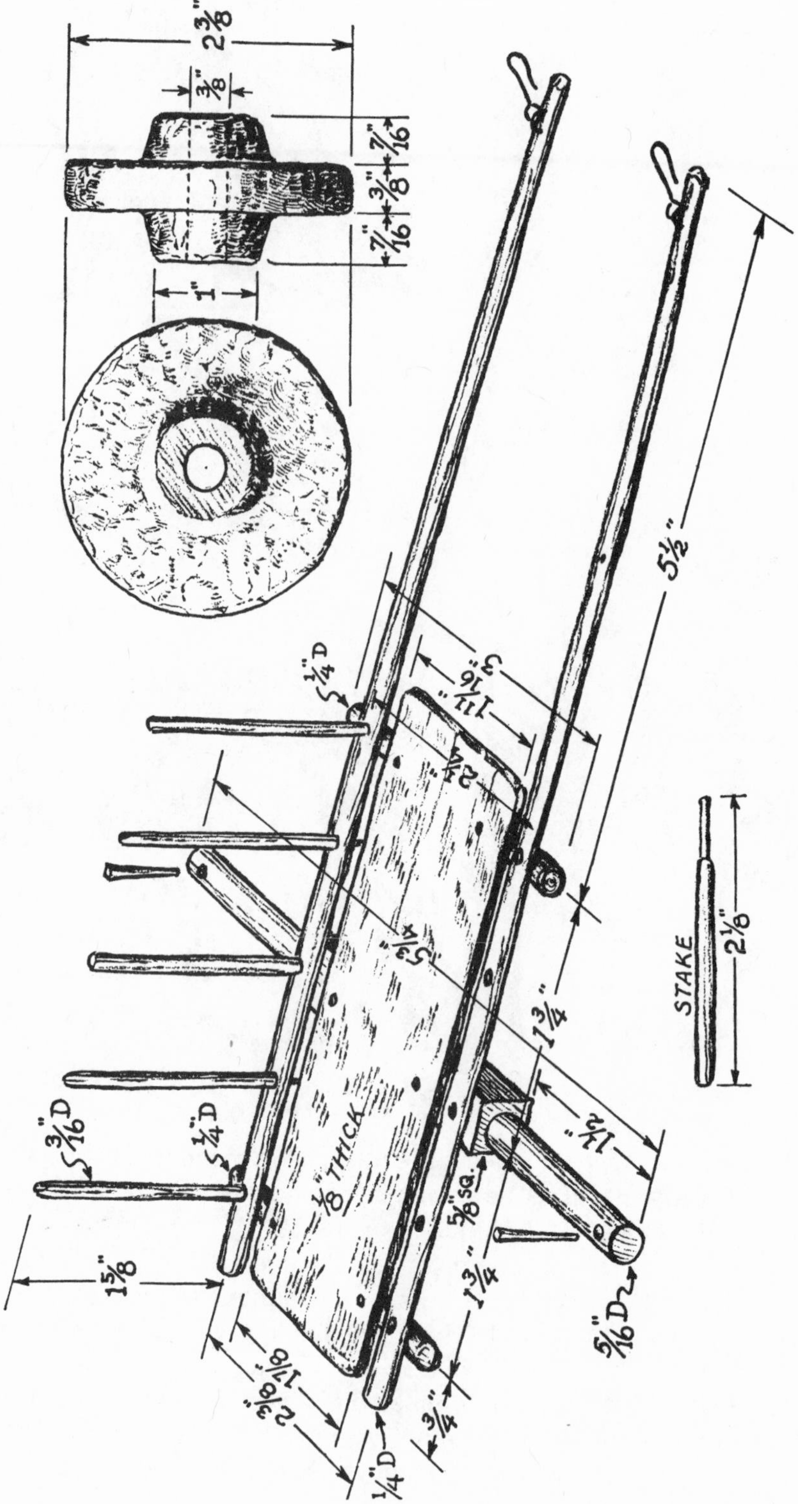

FIGURE 170. Details of the oxcart.

44   A Pack Mule

In the pack mule shown in Figure 171, you whittle the different objects in the mule's pack separately and then fit them all together. When you whittle the mule, cut out the silhouette from a piece of softwood, block it out, and then whittle. Use a sharp pocketknife and a crooked knife. A loaded pack

FIGURE 171.   Fully packed.

mule should be completed in a few evenings' time. The pack mule may be kept in the rough as illustrated or sanded to obtain a smoother finish.

The pack saddle, tools, utensils, and packs (see Figure 174) can be whittled out of scrap pieces. The pack saddle is made up of six pieces. The coffee pot is a solid piece of wood and the frying pan is hollowed out. The pickax is made of two pieces to avoid the narrow section of cross-grain, and the packs are simply two pieces of wood cut to resemble bundles of blankets and a tent. The pack saddle is fastened on with two thin bands of basswood bark, using a bit of glue to fasten the ends together. The ropes are made by twisting together fibers of the inner white bark. There is a small hole drilled between the ear and the neck for the halter.

Figure 171 shows how the mule is loaded. Fastening the pack onto the mule is much easier than trying to whittle the whole figure, mule and all, from one piece. Some may wish to burden their mule with another kind of load, such as camping and hunting equipment, or just a load of wood. If you wish to load the mule with wood, get a bundle of 2¾- and 3-inch twigs, some crooked and some straight, and trim the bark off.

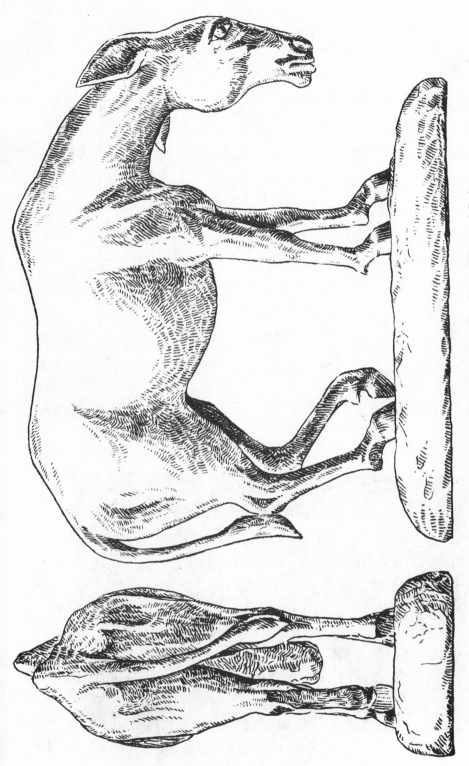

FIGURE 173.   Rear and right-hand views of pack mule.   All patterns are full-size.

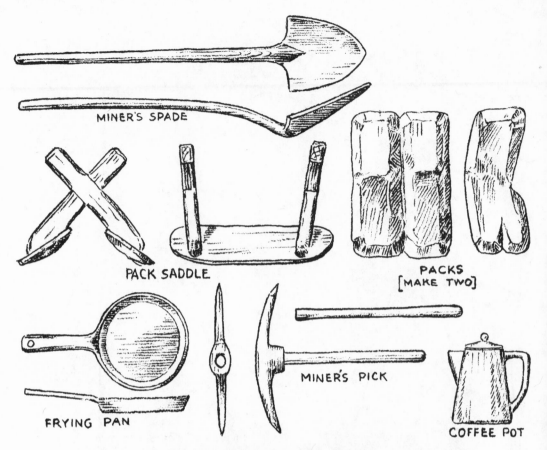

MINER'S SPADE

PACK SADDLE

PACKS
[MAKE TWO]

FRYING PAN

MINER'S PICK

COFFEE POT

FIGURE 174.   Details of pack.

FIGURE 175.   Ready to be packed.

Special Projects

45 Whittled Jewelry

For something different, you might like to try your hand at whittling jewelry. This chapter shows birds, fish, insects, Kachina dolls, and masks made into attractive pins, earrings, necklaces, belts, zipper pulls, and buttons. The Kachina doll necklace shown in Figure 176 would be a delight for any girl or woman. Feel free to make a pin for a man, and if you do, call it a lapel pin. And you will no doubt have many ideas for jewelry in addition to the ones shown in this chapter.

FIGURE 176. Full-size pattern of Kachina doll necklace.

The cardinal bird earring set is easily whittled and colored. The back of the pieces should be flat. Paint the birds bright red with a few markings as indicated in Figure 180.

The Kachina dolls are made like those described in an earlier chapter. If you make a Kachina doll pin, or zipper pull, the back should be made flat. For the necklace, five dolls are used. Make the center doll a little longer than the other four. In making zipper pulls and necklaces, you should give each doll an extension of wood at the top for an eyelet, as shown in Figure 176 and in A, Figure 177. Or, a small screw eye may be inserted into the top

Zipper Pull
A

Lamp Switch or
Shade Pull
B

FIGURE 177.

of the doll as shown in B, Figure 177. The beads, necklace string, and clasp for the necklace can be purchased at a variety store.

The belt shown in Figure 178 and the necklace shown in Figure 179 are simple to fasten, and usually held together with a cord for which holes must be drilled through the units with a 1/16-inch twist drill. Make the hole as close to the reverse side of the unit as is possible without splitting the wood. In

FIGURE 178. Belt.

FIGURE 179. The necklace.

view of this danger of splitting, the practical thing to do is to drill the holes into the blank units before you start to whittle. For the necklace, drill only one hole through the top. The units should be ¼ inch thick. When you string these pieces together, knot the cord after each one or insert beads into the spaces between them. For bracelets, use round or cord elastic, so that they may be slipped over the hand.

The butterflies are a little harder to whittle than the other subjects because the wings must be trimmed thin. The butterflies illustrated in Figure 180 are of the buckeye variety, and any book on butterflies will show how to paint them.

If made into earrings, the butterflies and the Kachina dolls belong to a set, but only one drawing is shown for each of them since the right and left

FIGURE 180. The finished lapel pins or earrings.

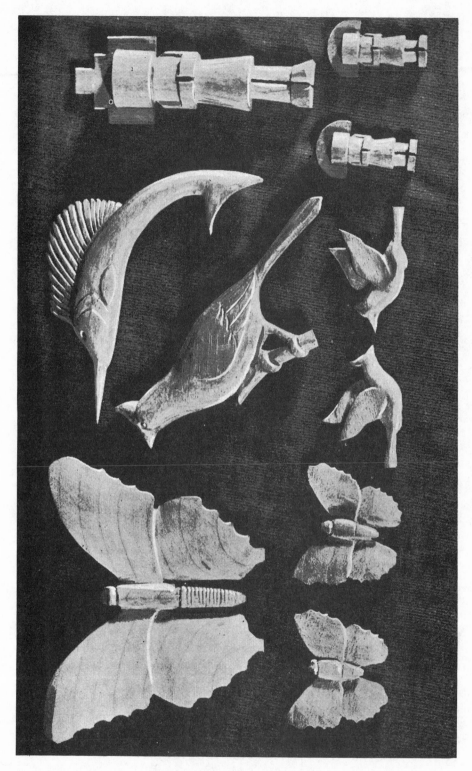

FIGURE 181. The sanded lapel pins or earrings.

earrings are exactly alike. The birds, however, must both face forward when worn as earrings, so two bird patterns are shown in Figure 182.

The sailfish is made and colored like the one shown in Figure 143, Chapter 35, except that it is flat at the back. Do not make earrings from the sailfish pattern, as they do not look well on the ears. All articles should be painted with watercolors and then given two or three coats of clear fingernail polish.

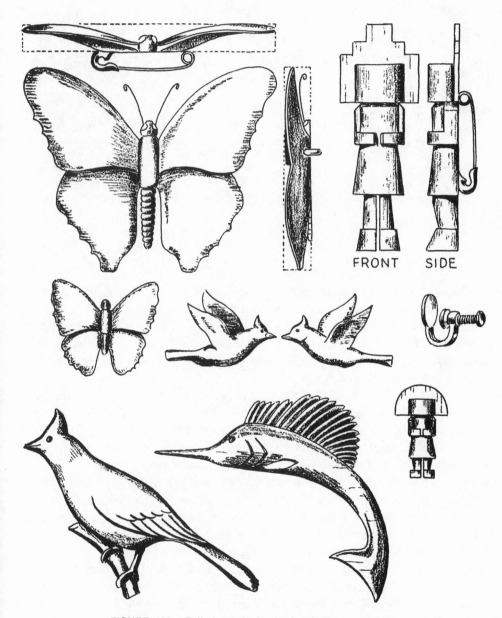

FIGURE 182. Full-size patterns for lapel pins or earrings.

The mask shown in Figure 183 should be whittled out of ⅝-inch wood. If walnut, mahogany, or cherry is used, the mask can be finished in the following manner: paint the eyes white with green pupils, the eyebrows black, and the lips red. Two or three coats of clear fingernail polish, applied after the watercolors are dry, will give the wood a beautiful flesh color.

FIGURE 183.   Full-size pattern for mask lapel pin.

Now to say a bit about fasteners. In Figure 182 there is a sketch of an earring fastener. These can be purchased at a variety store. They are made of plastic or metal and glued to the earrings with a waterproof cement. Sometimes the part of the fastener to be attached to the ornament must be cut down so it will not project over the edges of the ornament. This is often the case with Kachina doll earrings.

The simplest way to fasten the pins to a coat or dress is with an ordinary safety pin, the size depending upon the ornament. A, Figure 184, shows how the notch, or groove, is to be cut into the back of the ornament. The safety pin should fit snugly and be set into the wood a little less than halfway (see B, Figure 184). After it has been fitted, remove the pin from the groove, fill the groove with liquid or aluminum solder, and press the pin down into it again. If necessary, add a little more solder to fill the groove level with the surface. Then let the solder dry. Plastic wood may be used in the same manner. For long designs, such as totem poles and Kachinas, the pin should be placed lengthwise, as shown in C, Figure 184.

If a clasp fastening is wanted, buy a cheap clasp brooch at the dime store, remove the clasp, and cement it to the back of the whittled brooch with aluminum solder. Exact directions cannot be given here because of the many different varieties of clasps on the market.

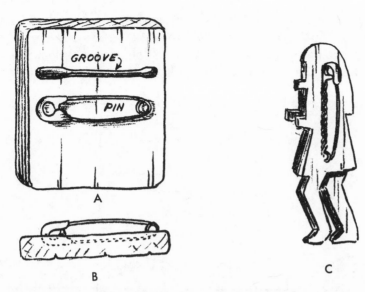

FIGURE 184. A, Attaching the safety pin to the block; B, setting the pin into the groove; C, fastening pin in a long design.

Buttons are attached by any one of the methods shown in Figure 185. The button shown in A has a depression whittled into the back. This button must be tied onto the garment. The reverse side of the button may also be whittled as shown in B, Figure 185, so that the button can be sewed on. Another method is shown in C, Figure 185, where a small D ring is set into a groove in the back of the button and cemented with liquid solder in the way described for the lapel pins and brooches.

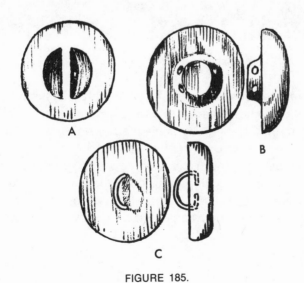

FIGURE 185.

In Figures 186 and 187 are shown the steps required to whittle beetle or scarab buttons. As they are rather small, they should be made of some harder wood than is ordinarily used for whittling. Birch, maple, or lemonwood are easy to whittle, for they have very little grain. Many kinds of beetles are very

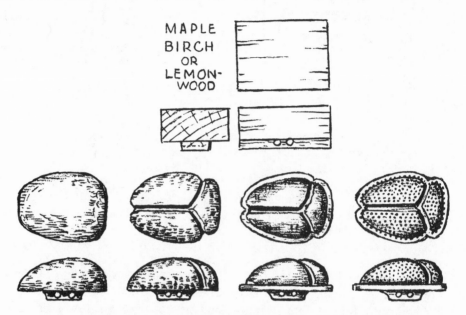

FIGURE 186. Full-size patterns for the beetle button.

FIGURE 187. Successive steps in the carving of a button.

colorful and have interesting shapes. Look for colored illustrations in books on insects. The one shown here has a bright metallic-green back, and the edge is a metallic red. The little dots are made with the blunt end of an awl, after the beetle is sanded and before it is painted. A small amount of aluminum powder may be mixed with the watercolors to get the desired metallic finish, and one coat of clear fingernail polish is given for the final finish. These buttons were made to be fastened through buttonholes. Where the buttons are to be used only for ornament, the beetles may be made larger and more elaborate, with feelers and legs.

46 Whittling Spirals

Anyone who does any amount of woodworking, and especially furniture making, will at some time or other wish to learn spiral whittling.

Commercially, spirals are made on spindle lathes. However, when one wants to decorate a piece of furniture and requires only a few spirals, they can be whittled in a very satisfactory manner. There is nothing difficult about it; it is simply a matter of cutting with the grain.

The single spiral or corkscrew is the easiest to make. The simplest method of laying it out on the stick is with a long, narrow strip of paper. The paper should be an even width, and if the stick is a perfect cylinder, it will space itself evenly as shown in Figure 188. Fasten the ends with a pin or tack, then mark out the spiral along the edges with a pencil. Figure 189 shows how a piece of wire, the coils of which have been carefully spaced with a rule, may be used in laying out a spiral.

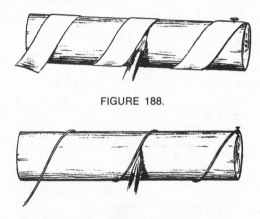

FIGURE 188.

FIGURE 189.

To lay out a double spiral, use a paper strip as shown in Figure 190, or lay it out as shown in Figure 191. For a 1⅛-inch diameter stick, the cross-lines shown in the drawing should be 1½ inches apart. Mark with a pencil. To lay out an open spiral, use the same method as shown for the double spiral (see Figure 190).

If the outer edges of the spirals are to be sharp, only one line is required. If the edges are to be cut to a certain width, a second line should be drawn,

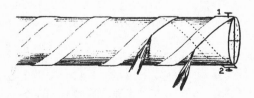

FIGURE 190.

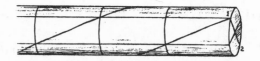

FIGURE 191.

running parallel to the one marked first, and about ⅛ inch from it. Figure 192 shows how the stick should look, marked for a single spiral.

To start whittling, the easiest method is making a shallow V cut the full length of the stick. If a double spiral is to be cut, whittle the two cuts. Do

FIGURE 192.

not cut right up to the pencil line (see Figure 193). Hold the knife as shown in Figure 26, page 12. The, using the methods shown in Figures 25, 26, and 27, whittle until the spiral looks like Figures 194 and 195. Cut right up to the pencil lines and keep the ridge even.

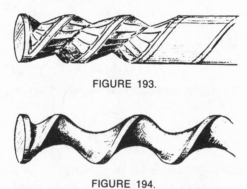

FIGURE 193.

FIGURE 194.

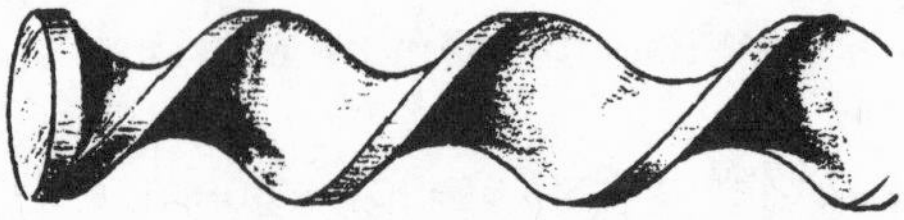

FIGURE 195.

Whittle first one side and then the other, ending the last cut at the bottom, where the grain is straight. If a smooth-finished spiral is desired, finish with sandpaper wrapped around a round stick as shown in Figure 196.

Figure 197 shows a peace-pipe stem made with a double spiral. On this stem the spiral has a twist running from left to right. This is just as simple to whittle as one that twists in the opposite direction.

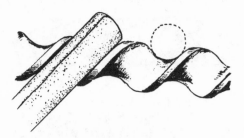

FIGURE 196.

FIGURE 197.

Figure 198 shows the Jacobean spiral. which is used a great deal in furniture and balusters.

FIGURE 198.

Lay out for a single spiral and start with a V cut as shown in Figure 199, going the full length of the part to be whittled. Then go over the whole groove with a deeper cut, as shown at the right end of Figure 199, being careful to keep an even depth. From then on it is just a simple job to round the spirals. The twisted spirals should be carefully sanded, but if they have been whittled neatly and carefully, they will look well without sanding.

FIGURE 199.

The square spiral—that is, a spiral cut from a square piece of wood—was used a great deal by the old Spanish settlers, who did not have access to lathes. Some of the very attractive work of these early pioneers can still be seen in the southwest.

Figure 200 shows a finished piece of square spiral with a long pitch. Lay out the square as shown in Figure 202. After laying it out, make the V cuts on all the slant lines as shown in Figure 201. Follow with a second cut

FIGURE 200.

FIGURE 201.

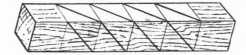

FIGURE 202.

as shown at the right side of Figure 201, taking off the shoulder at the same time. It will be noticed that the bottom points of the V cuts do not meet at the corners. To bring them in line, a smaller V cut must be made at a greater slant at the corners. After that, the finishing is practically the same as for any other rounded spiral.

One more that should be added to this series is a tapered spiral. Naturally, if the stick is tapered, the spiral, to be consistent, should taper also. In other words, the intervals of the spiral should get shorter as the smaller end of the stick is approached.

To lay out a tapered spiral, draw equally spaced lines lengthwise. Starting at the larger end, take one half of the diameter at that point and draw the first crossline, *a,* that distance from the starting point, as shown in Figure 203. Then measure the diameter at *a* and draw the next line, *b*, one half of that diameter from *a*, and continue this to the end of the spiral. The spirals

FIGURE 203.

are then laid out like any of the others; and, of course, the whittling is also the same, whether it be rounded, hollow, or open. Figure 204 shows a hollow or concave tapered spiral.

FIGURE 204.

When whittling an open spiral, like the one shown in Figures 205 and 206, cut it the same as the double spiral, the full length of both grooves. Then take a second cut, cutting the sides steeper; perhaps a third cut will be required before the V cuts meet in the center of the stick. From now on, care must be taken and the grain must be watched. Hold the stick and knife as shown in Figure 205 to cut away the surplus core. Cut down the full length as shown, and then cut down on the other side.

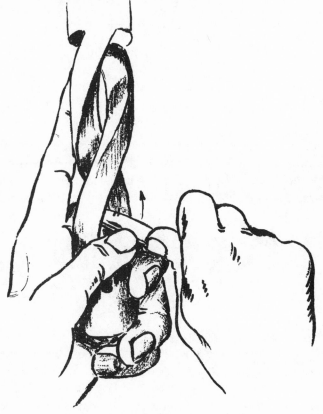

FIGURE 205.

Figure 206 shows an open spiral cut from a basswood limb. This was used for a rattle handle. While only single and double spirals are shown and described here, triple or quadruple spirals may also be cut. To lay out such spirals, simply divide the end of the stick into three or four parts as shown in

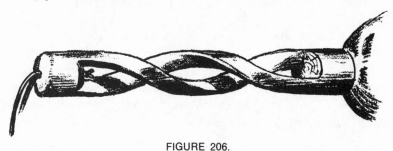

FIGURE 206.

Figure 207, then proceed in the same manner as was described for laying out single and double spirals.

Spirals may be cut deep or shallow, depending on what they are to be used for. The deeper-cut spirals have more grace and the shallow-cut

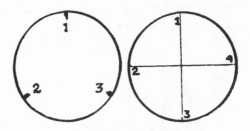

FIGURE 207.

spirals have more strength. Whittling spirals is fun, once the art has been mastered, and they can be incorporated in a great many articles of furniture.

Figure 208 shows a rounded spiral that is just the opposite of those shown in Figures 194 and 195, which are more or less hollowed out.

FIGURE 208.

Lay out the spiral, whether single or double, as shown in Figures 188 to 190. Use a single line for the single twist, or two lines for the double. Notice that the pitch of the spiral in Figure 209 is less than those shown in Figures 194 and 195.

The pitch or slant, of course, is optional, but it also depends on what the particular piece is to be used for or how much work the whittler wishes to undertake. Start with a V cut as shown in Figure 209. Probably this will have to be cut deeper with a second V cut, depending upon the size of the

FIGURE 209.

work. Then, with smaller cuts, round up the work nicely; if you like, finish with sandpaper. Figure 208 shows a double spiral; when finished it should look like two vines twisting around each other.

47 Turtle Paperweight

This paperweight is a whittled example of the North American box turtle. This is a land turtle which is able to shut itself completely within its shell—which is why it is called a box turtle.

FIGURE 210.   Sanded turtle above; the turtle with its final decoration below.

The first step in making your box turtle is to mark the top view of the turtle, as shown at the upper right in Figure 211, on a piece of 1½- by 2¾-inch white pine or other suitable wood. Place it so that the grain of the wood runs lengthwise.   Then saw out the silhouette as shown.

The next step is to cut straight down along the edge of the shell to the heights given for the legs, feet, and tail, also shown at the upper right in Figure 211.   Round up the shell, and use ⅙-inch V cuts to outline the shell sections.   After finishing the head and feet, sand the whole piece carefully. Then bore holes in the bottom and fill them with lead or Babbitt metal to give weight to the little reptile.

The painting of the shell has been simplified somewhat (see Figure 210), but it is similar to the real turtle's colors. Paint the background a deep reddish brown and the smaller areas yellow, with light brown edges and crosslines to soften up the design. Paint the legs, head, and tail grey, with a greenish line running from the nose over the eye and ending right back of the eyes. Then give the shell a couple of coats of clear nail polish for a finish.

The silhouette

FIGURE 211.   Full-size pattern for the box turtle.

48 Horse-head and Buffalo-head Book Ends

The animal-head book ends shown in Figure 212 are modern in style and extremely handsome. When you see how attractive these book ends look on your bookcase, you will realize the full satisfaction of practicing the art of whittling. And they make wonderful gifts.

FIGURE 212. Horse-head and buffalo-head book ends.

Draw the full-size patterns shown in Figures 213 and 214 on a block of wood. Cut out the silhouettes and rough out the general outlines. The animals' muscles should be sharply defined and carved in a simplified style. The hair in the mane of the horse and the heavy wool of the buffalo are finished in smooth masses. These book ends should be sanded down carefully to look their best.

The horseshoe backs shown in Figure 215 are sawed out of a ¾- or ⅞-inch piece of board. Figure 212 shows the finished assembly of the book ends, and Figure 216 shows the detailed assembly.

In order to give weight to the book ends, holes should be bored into the back of the buffalo head and the bottom of the horse head, and then filled with lead or Babbitt metal.

Each of the horse-head book ends consists of four pieces: the head, the horseshoe, the backing for the horseshoe, and the base. The different parts should be glued together and also fastened with small flathead screws.

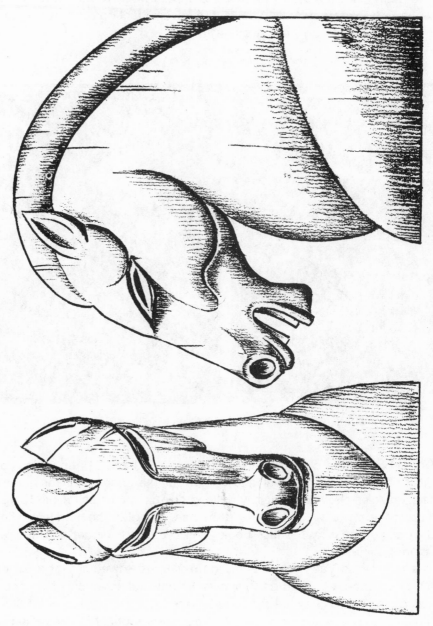

FIGURE 213. Full-size pattern of horse-head book ends.

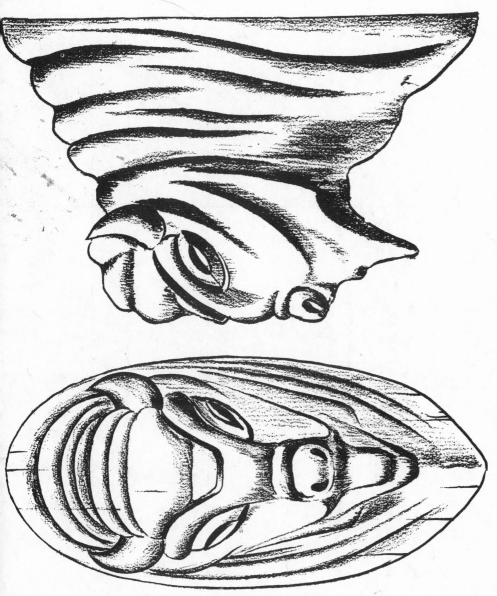

FIGURE 214. Full-size pattern of buffalo book ends.

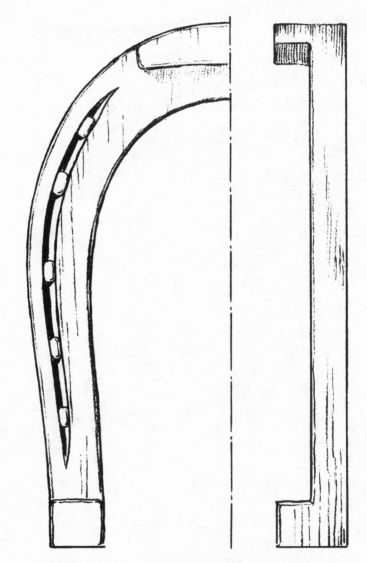

FIGURE 215.   Horseshoe back for the book ends.

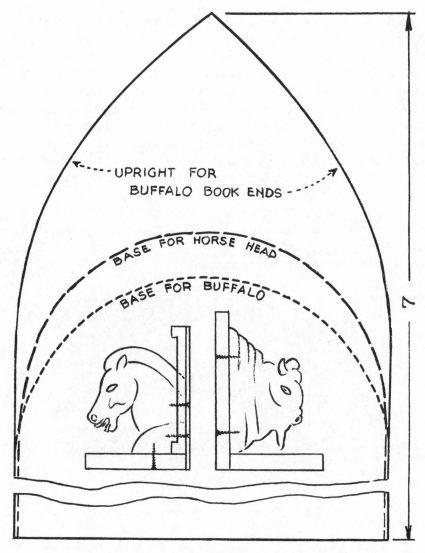

FIGURE 216.   Assembling the book ends.

If felt is glued to the ends and bottom of the base, the screws may be left flush; otherwise they should be covered with plastic wood. If you are working with a clear-grained wood, a light or dark stain may be used. After the stain has dried, the book ends may be given a coat of either dull or glossy varnish.

If the grain of the wood is not so attractive, two or three coats of cream or ivory enamel will give the book ends the appearance of fine china.

49 Salad Fork and Spoon

A salad fork and spoon set is another project you might like to whittle. I have chosen a fish pattern for the handles of my set. In the full-size example in Figure 220, the fish is shown only once. If you wish, carve the fish in one position on the fork and then reverse it on the spoon.

Carve the set from two pieces of rather hard wood, 1¼ by 2 by 10¼ inches. Probably the best wood would be maple, although this is rather hard to whittle. Birch cuts more easily and is the material out of which most commercial salad forks and spoons are made. Walnut and mahogany may also be used, but a filler must be applied on both of these woods to close the pores and give the salad set a smooth finish. Lemonwood or cherry could likewise be used for this project.

To prepare the blank, Figure 217, cut out the silhouette, using the side view as the pattern as shown in Figure 220. Then trace the top view on the silhouette just sawed out, and cut off the waste wood. This procedure saves considerable time in the actual whittling.

FIGURE 217. Blanks for salad fork and spoon.

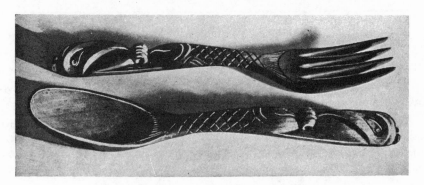

FIGURE 218. The finished salad set.

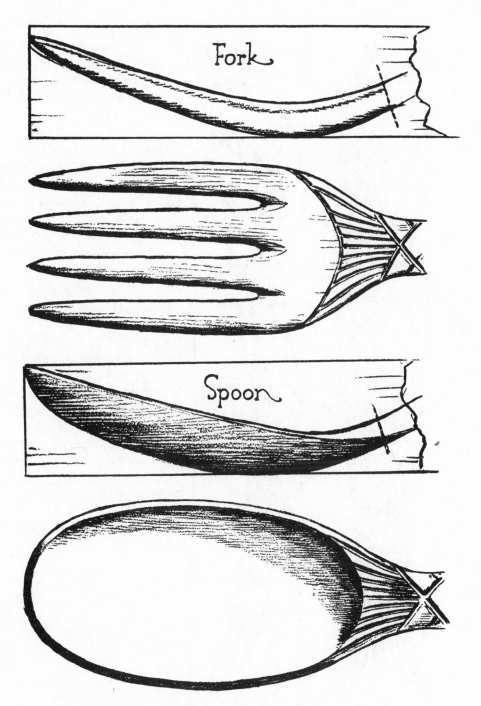

FIGURE 219. Full-size pattern of the salad fork and spoon.

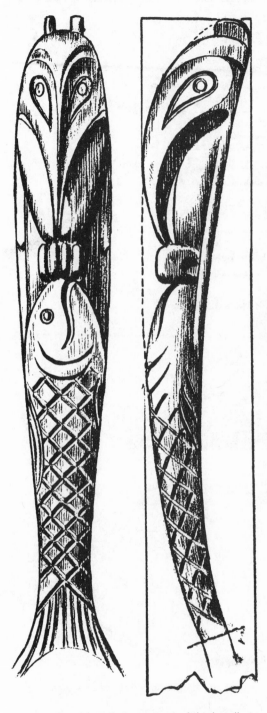

The crooked knife shown in Figure 11 was used to carve out the bowl of the spoon. If a knife of this kind is not available, a gouge will have to be used, as a pocketknife cannot do this job.

After the whittling has been completed, the fork and spoon may be left with the knife marks showing, or they may be sanded down smoothly. If walnut or mahogany has been used, a suitable paste filler must be applied first. The filler, when dry, must be followed by a sealing coat of thin white shellac, and after that is dry the project should be rubbed down carefully with steel wool. Two coats of varnish, rubbed down with crude oil and pumice stone, will complete the finishing operation.

Other methods of finishing also might be used: two coats of clear lacquer could be applied; or if the fork and spoon are made of fine-grained wood, they might be given a series of well-rubbed coats of salad oil until a fine natural finish is effected.

FIGURE 220. Full-size pattern of the handle to be used for fork and spoon.

50 A Set of Whittled Chessmen

Moderately priced chessmen are either turned on a lathe or they are cast. The very expensive ones are carved or whittled.

It is not a difficult task to whittle a beautiful set of chessmen, and it can be done in a few evenings. Use a small-bladed knife that has been properly sharpened.

The first thing to decide is whether the men are to be made of softwood or of hardwood. Since the pieces are small and do not require too much work, it may be well to choose hardwood, so that continued use will not nick and dent them. Birch or maple may be used for making the white men, and walnut or mahogany for the black men. To make one set darker, a coat or two of walnut stain may be applied. Of course, all of the men may be

FIGURE 221. The completed set of chessmen.

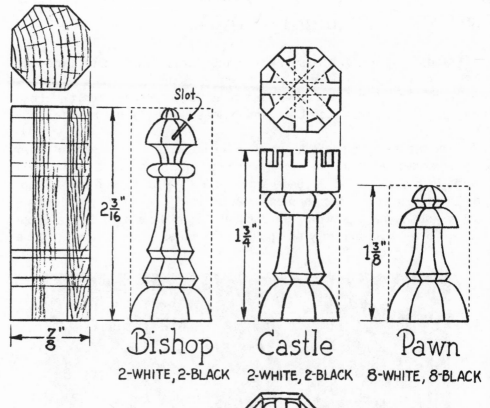

Slot

$2\frac{3}{16}$"

$\frac{7}{8}$"

Bishop

2-WHITE, 2-BLACK

$1\frac{3}{4}$"

Castle

2-WHITE, 2-BLACK

$1\frac{3}{8}$"

Pawn

8-WHITE, 8-BLACK

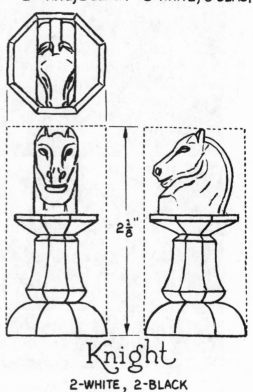

$2\frac{1}{8}$"

Knight

2-WHITE, 2-BLACK

FIGURE 222. Chessmen.

whittled out of birchwood, and then one of the sets may be painted with a coat of flat black paint. The final finish may consist of several coats of clear varnish or lacquer.

If the sets are made of softwood, such as bass, the whittling will take less time, and the chessmen will still be quite serviceable.

The simplest way to start is to cut strips of wood to octagonal shape on the circular saw. These pieces should then be planed with a sharp plane. About 2 feet of the 1-inch stock and 2 feet of the 7/8-inch stock will be used for each color. This will allow for some spoilage.

Mark off the divisions and whittle the shapes shown in Figure 222. The eye will quickly detect whether the cuts have been correctly make. One who has done little or no whittling should make a few trial cuts, going all the way around the stick. It is really surprising how easy the chessmen are to whittle and how quickly they can be made. Be sure to have the bottoms squared off properly. Cut all blanks to length with a power saw, or in a

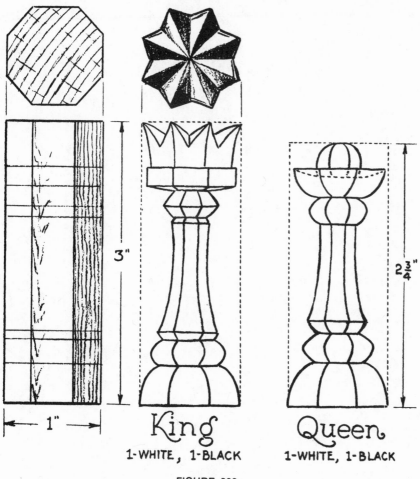

King
1-WHITE, 1-BLACK

Queen
1-WHITE, 1-BLACK

FIGURE 223.

miter box, before starting to whittle. The bottoms also may be squared off on a sanding disk. Be sure that they all stand properly, because after they are finished it will be a lot harder to get them to stand straight.

Finishing the chessmen is a matter of personal taste. The knife cuts may be left as they are, or the pieces may be sanded before they are varnished (see Figure 221). For sanding, fasten a strip of fine sandpaper to a piece of galvanized iron with waterglass glue or shellac. Use this method in the same manner as you would use a thin knife file. This permits sanding all the deeper cuts. Also, you may want to glue felt to the bottom of each piece.